AF423968

Sing a **new** Song

CHRISTON KESSINGER

Sing a New Song

Christon Kessinger

© 2023

Publisher: IngramSpark

Editor: Sherry Chamblee

Cover Designer: Katrina D. Ronneburger

Title Designer: Annie Lee Kessinger

ISBN: 979-8-218-27468-9

Printed in USA

This is a true story, although some names may have been changed to protect the identities of those involved.

let the whole earth
sing to the lord!

sing to the lord;
praise his name.

each day proclaim the
good news that he saves.
publish his glorious deeds
among the nations.

tell everyone about the
amazing things he does.

(Psalm 96:1-3 NLT)

this book is dedicated to my husband troy
who has given me the life i always
dreamed of...

contents

Melodies have been pulsing through my veins since utero as my father was a musician, singer, songwriter in the 1960's. Each chapter begins with a song whose lyrics helped me survive during that particular season of life. I do not have permission to use their lyrics in written form in my story, so I have linked you to the artist's official music video. You can either use the QR code or the link below to access the playlist. Enjoy!

https://linktr.ee/christonkessinger

foreword

by Troy Kessinger

It was a February night in 1992. This was my third blind date over the last few months and I was beginning to think my friends hated me. The women I was being set up with were not my type at all. Why I chose to listen to one of my high school students is baffling but he was so convinced that a new nurse in town, who attended his church, was the perfect woman for me. Promising myself that this would be the last blind date I would ever agree to, I reluctantly knocked on the door. As the door opened, I heard a gentle whisper say, "This is the one you've been praying for."

This beautiful woman turned my life upside down. She was fun, intelligent and most importantly loved Jesus with all her heart. Like the peeling of an onion, she slowly revealed parts of her life that had been difficult and painful. With each shocking layer I fell in love with her even more. This woman's life was different from everyone in her family and Jesus was to blame. Nine months after our first date, she had my heart and my last name.

To be honest, watching her sift through old journals was difficult. I did not want her to return to those toxic, dysfunctional places. However, when she read me excerpts along the way, I was overwhelmed by the presence and grace of God in her life. I am so proud of Christon for listening to that same gentle whisper to put her story into words. Even after thirty years of marriage her story still gets to me emotionally and pushes me closer to my Savior.

seriously god?

I was never a good writer and English class gave me hives, so imagine my confusion when, shortly after my mother passed away, I heard God whisper, "It is time to tell your story." True confessions, in high school my mom wrote most of my papers. My habit was to hand her a quickly scribbled rough draft and ask her to proofread it. Of course it was atrocious, so she would spend hours correcting and then typing "her" masterpiece. Writing in the 1980's was just too much work. There were no computers or internet to assist in your research. We had to use resources we kept on a shelf called dictionaries and musky outdated encyclopedias. Typing a paper on a typewriter was a pain in the hiney too. Correcting errors in a paragraph might mean a total redo of the paper unless the gobs of white-out dried perfectly, allowing the typewriter ink not to smear. My first reaction to God's nudge to write was to remind Him of why I clearly was not fit for this task.

My Journal:
January 2014
Dear God,
Can I be honest? I really don't want to write my story down on paper. So many reasons why I shouldn't flood my mind: One, I am a lousy writer. Two, I don't want to relive it. Three, let's be real, I have no time to sit. Four, who is really going to care? Other people have far more exciting stories than mine. Can't they do it?

My devotion today was Exodus 4:10-13 (NLT). Moses pleaded with the Lord, "O Lord, I'm not very good with words. I never have been, and I'm not now, even though you have spoken to me. I get tongue-tied and my words get tangled." Then the Lord asked Moses, "Who makes a person's mouth? Who decides whether people speak or do not speak, hear or do not hear, see or do not see? Is it not I the Lord? Now go! I will be with you as you speak, and I will instruct you in what to say." But Moses again pleaded, "Lord, please! Send someone else."

I wish I could tell you that I was obedient and jumped right on it. Unfortunately, I ignored God. A year later, I was still making excuses. Surely God would not ask me to do something I was totally incapable of performing. The only explanation for my perceived hearing impairment was a physical disorder. Clearly, I had been stricken with early menopausal hormone imbalance causing a lapse in mental stability. God never gave up.

My Journal:
May 2015
*I was sent an invitation to be an honored guest at a Hospice
luncheon at our local hospital. Their staff had been in
our home twice in the last few years as both my mother
and my husband's mother battled with pancreatic cancer.
Emotionally not ready to process my own grief, I threw the
invitation away. A day before the event I received a phone
call from the event coordinator explaining the itinerary of
the afternoon. Our mothers were being honored by nurses
and caretakers who had spent valuable time loving them.
How could I blow it off?*

*As I drove to the hospital the next morning, I heard God
whisper, "Get a journal today and begin writing." Literally
seconds later, the DJ on K-Love introduced a new release by
Big Daddy Weave called My Story. The words to this song
were as if God himself were singing them to me.*

*I entered the hospital with no makeup on, a hot mess!
It warmed my heart to see so many familiar faces and hear
their stories of how our mothers had touched their lives.
After the closing prayer, I gathered my purse and bolted
out the door, hoping to avoid small talk or any more tears.
I was halfway down the hallway when I heard someone call
my name. The Hospice coordinator handed me a beautiful
gift basket filled with goodies. Sticking out of the top was a
journal and pen. Seriously God?*

It dawned on me that I had it all wrong! My insecurities were causing me to miss the journey God wanted to walk me through, fixating on my inability to see the purpose. My mind was consumed with unanswered questions: would it be for my children, a future Bible study, or kindling for our next bonfire? The thought of digging up the past kept me paralyzed from simply obeying God. One evening I had an epiphany: This was not about me at all, this was God's story. I did not need to look at this assignment through my old lenses of brokenness, rejection, and pain, but through my new ones of redemption, forgiveness, and healing. For I am a new creation, the old is gone. (2 Corinthians 5:17) Thank you, God, for pushing me out of my comfort zone. *Take note, God always wins!*

My story reveals how I was born into a family that for generations was dysfunctional. Addictions, abuse, secrets, and lies hovered like a dark cloud over every family member. My mother's unexpected pregnancy with me was actually a blessing to some degree as it rescued her, at least temporarily, from a life of drugs. This was why she often referred to me as her "angel child." She did her best to protect me, making sure that foul language was curbed and consumption hidden whenever I was present. Everything changed when I became a teenager. My fairy tale family was shattered into shards of broken glass. Consumed with confusion, I caved, participating in activities that numbed the pain, if only for a moment. Naturally, in my mind I justified these behaviors since the adults in my life coped the same way. The momentary amnesia was only a band-aid on a festering wound, leaving me filled with guilt and shame. Through providential circumstances and unexpected friendships, Jesus showed up and my life would never be the same.

you might look like them,
you might live with them,
but
you don't have to act like them,
you don't have to love like them,
you can
sing a new song.

♡

who's driving this train

Barry Ray

My mother left behind decades of handwritten journals documenting her life and some of her deepest insecurities and pain. It was a treasure to find letters that I didn't know existed, tucked between the pages of her writings. As I sifted through them alongside my own journals, emotions and memories of events resurfaced. Revisiting these memories was difficult, as I now viewed them through different perspectives: the younger me, the adult me, the wife me, and the mommy me. Many of my family members are gone now and it pains me to think of their talents, gifts, and legacies wasted.

Tragedy, pain, and darkness all have the power to destroy us. They can leave us in a muddy puddle, useless and ineffective, or they can propel us to make a difference in this life. When I finally laid down my hurt and my heart, God showed up and changed everything. Little did I know, He had been singing over me all along. (Zephaniah 3:17)

My mother, Linda Marie, was born October 25, 1944 in Wichita, TX. She was the oldest of three, and the only daughter of Joan Margaret (Gagga) and Dr. Thomas Smith (Poppi), a Lt Col and oral surgeon in the United States Air Force. Her younger brothers were Thomas (Tom), and Robert (Bo). Shortly after Linda graduated from high school in 1962, her parents were deployed to Japan, and my mother accompanied them. While there she enrolled in classes at Sophia University, modeled on the side, and worked for a year as a guest participant for a nationally popular radio program called "English for Millions." It was broadcast twice weekly on a nationwide hook-up from Station JOQR (Japan Cultural Broadcasting Corporation) in Tokyo. The show also aired on television three times a week on Station NET channel 10, and nationwide on 24 other stations. She was known to millions who tuned into the radio and television programs throughout Japan. Her parents thought she would receive a better education in the states, sending her to Oklahoma where she had extended family. She attended Oklahoma State University (OSU), majoring in Physical Education. Her choice of majors was puzzling when the following excerpt from her boss in Japan shows her interest in television or radio. She also loved creative writing and dreamed of publishing children's books. In hindsight, a degree in English, Journalism, or Communications seems more her personality.

Excerpt from letter:
To: Linda
From: J.B. Harris, editorial advisor for Obunsha Company
If American producers fail to discover you they must be as blind as bats. Everybody here knows that you're a natural TV and radio talent.

One evening, during her senior year at OSU, she and a few friends strolled over to Gino's, a bar near campus, to listen to Martha's Vineyard, a local band from Stillwater, Oklahoma. My mother was mesmerized by the talent of their lead singer, Barry Ray. They dated briefly, marrying in a private ceremony without her parent's blessing. This was heartbreaking to her parents, especially since she was the only girl. Their disappointment was heightened when she dropped out of her last semester of college to pursue Barry's dream of becoming a recorded musician.

The entire band, with their girlfriends, moved to Southern California and and rented a small house. This was 1968 when the Communal Hippie Movement was the rage. The girls worked to support the band so the guys could focus on their music and upcoming record deal. In 1969, the album *Plain Jane* was released, featuring ten original tracks with all four band members contributing. There was a financial dispute between management and the studio, and sadly, an album which was released prior to *Plain Jane* was lost forever.

Then, surprise... Linda became pregnant, with me! Not exactly great timing. The insecurity of becoming a father, a pending record contract, financial worries, combined with being newly married, all made for toxic times. Barry became disconnected and began camouflaging his fears by drowning himself in alcohol and drugs. Irrational paranoia set in, accusing his pregnant wife of having an affair and his band members of conspiracy. He had convinced himself that they were trying to oust him from the band.

The birth of a healthy baby girl, Christon (AKA: Christy, Chris, Twinkie, Angel) on February 3, 1969 did nothing to reprioritize what was important. Barry's bizarre behaviors only escalated. For over a year, my mother endured his crazy mood swings, along with the shady people he brought into their home. Filled with trepidation over what he might do in one of his drug induced states, she packed me up and we flew to her parents in Panama City, Florida. Initially, she hoped our visit would only be for a week, propelling Barry to get his act together. Unfortunately, weeks turned into months. My mother saved many of the letters written by Sydney, a girlfriend of one of the band members. They were filled with tales of Barry's erratic lifestyle and lies, numerous times advising her to move on and forget him. The lie that hurt the most was when Barry began telling friends and family that I was not his child.

A few months after we left California, Barry returned to his parents, Becky and Bill, in Oklahoma, broke and alone. They wrote a few letters giving updates on Barry's condition.

> *Excerpt from letter:*
> *To: Linda*
> *From: Becky*
> *Linda, let's face it, Barry is sick, sick, sick in mind and body.*
> *Hell, it was not our Barry that came home, it was the Devil.*
> *He talks filthy and says weird things, then will bury his head*
> *and cry saying, "I love her, I love her!"*

Some of the letters portray Becky as an enabling mother that hoped, however unrealistic, that her love would pull him out of his psychosis. Another letter informed Linda that Barry had burned their marriage license, given away all their possessions, and moved to Canada with another woman. His father, Bill, on the other hand, was disgusted with his son and attempted to use tough love tactics. An argument over Barry wanting money results in his father telling him, "Get out and make your own!"

Excerpt from letter:
To: Linda
From: Bill
I feel as though I have lost a son and buried him.

Barry also wrote letters to my mother; however, most were illegible with rambling insane thoughts. My mother attempted to reconcile at one point, but to no avail. Her last letter was returned with "P.S. Barry has moved to Los Angeles, address is unknown" handwritten on the back. The divorce was finalized on December 9, 1970. The humility it took to admit to herself and to her parents that she had made a dreadful choice marrying Barry took a tremendous amount of courage. This must have been difficult since she avoided conflict and confrontation at all cost.

My grandparents, who I called Poppi and Gagga, relentlessly pressured my mother to let them adopt me. Often they criticized her parenting skills, saying, "Linda, you are not Christy's friend, you are her mother!" Poppi was approaching retirement and was talking about a possible last tour assignment to the Azores. Shortly after this news and a very emotionally draining year for my mom, she began lifeguarding at the public pool on Tyndall Air Force Base. There, she met CJ, a handsome enlisted gentleman. Shortly after their courtship began, the three of us moved to California. *I wonder now, did she leave so quickly with a man she barely knew out of fear that my grandparents would take me out of the country, or was it to escape their criticism and control?*

We would be in California less than a year when the relationship with CJ began to sour. The following letter from a friend exposes my mother's unhappiness.

One evening, my mother went to visit a girlfriend who lived in an apartment complex in North Hollywood. Running up the staircase, adjusting the slipping wine bottle in her arms, she unexpectedly collided into a gentleman carrying a loaf of bread. Jimm and my mother never arrived at their intended destinations. Instead, they casually sat on the stairs sharing bread, wine, and interesting conversation.

Christon and Linda

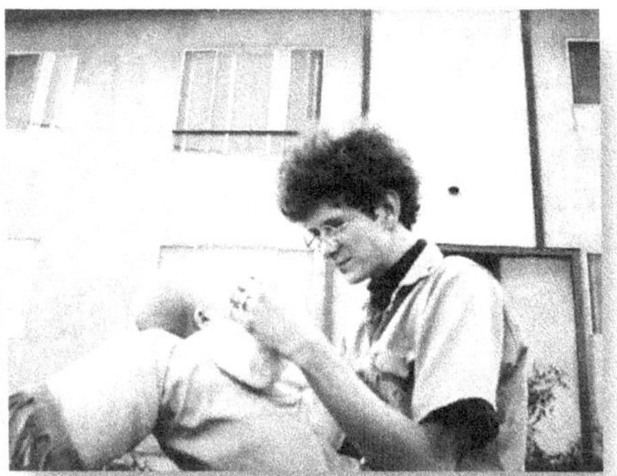

Christon and Barry

Plain Jane album,
Barry Ray [front middle]

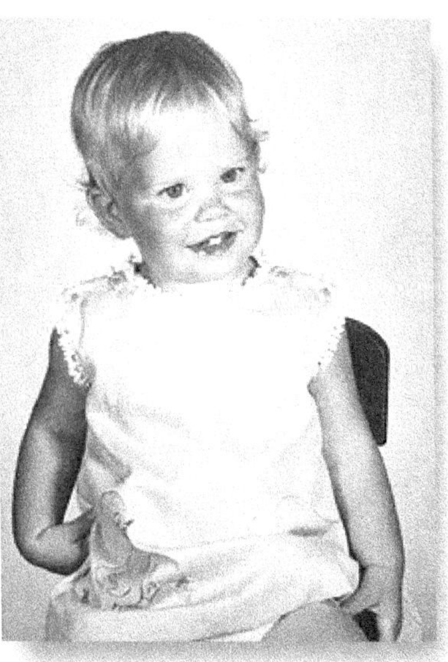

Christon - 15 months

Dr. Thomas Smith [Poppi]
and Joan Margaret [Gagga]

Linda pregnant

Linda modeling in Japan

Linda on Japanese
magazine cover.

chapel of love

Dixie Cups

My mother and Jimm's first official date was out to dinner with me, then four years old. I insisted on sitting beside him in the crowded restaurant. Shortly following dinner, with casual conversations flowing, I suddenly turned to Jimm in a piercing voice and shrieked, "God, you stink: Did you poop? It smells like diarrhea!" Although slightly blushing, he handled it like a trooper, quietly responding, "No, I am not guilty, but you are right, there is an awful odor in here. Let's leave, okay?" So much for first impressions! My unpredictable honesty did not derail their relationship; they were married a few months later, on July 4, 1974 in the Little Brown Church in North Hollywood.

Jimm's Journal:
4 July 1974 - Honeymoon Weekend
Hello World, Linda and I are officially Mr. and Mrs. I love her and want whatever makes her happy. Our drive up the coast from Los Angeles was nice. We stayed the weekend in Solvang, a little Danish town with cool weather and blue skies. A dramatic change from the brown smoggy skies and heat of L.A. We went bar hopping until midnight, then went to a restaurant for breakfast. I was so smashed! Somehow we

made it back to our hotel.

Woke up at noon, both feeling lousy. This place is larger than I had first thought. Lots of little shops and restaurants. We had a lovely day and took lots of photos.

Did a little sightseeing before heading back to L.A. after lunch. We stopped at one of the strangest towns, Isla Vista, very weird and dead. Got home about 6:30pm. Christy called me Daddy!

They rented a small white house on Goleta Street in the Valley. Before enrolling at Hadden Elementary, Jimm changed my last name on my birth certificate, adding his name as my legal father. I can still remember sitting at the large wooden dining room table squirming with excitement as he meticulously tampered with an official document. This would be considered paternal fraud, but for a 5-year-old little girl, it meant I finally had a Daddy. I had no idea that it was illegal or that this would be a foreshadowing of Jimm's lack of integrity.

We lived in an all Mexican neighborhood. Trying hard to fit in with my fellow kindergartners, I begged my mother to dye my hair black. I spoke with a perfectly mastered Chicano accent even though I knew very little Spanish. There was a little Hernandez girl who lived down the street who did not know English, so we made up our own language when we played after school.

There wasn't much money those early years, but we had each other and music. Whether we went camping for the weekend at Big Sur Lake, played at the park, swam at Haddon Dam, or grilled in the backyard, there was always music. So many sweet memories of my childhood involved our family jam sessions. Some nights, Jimm would be our DJ, spinning our favorite albums on the turntable while my mom and I danced around the room. Music had been pulsing through my veins in the womb, so it was no surprise when I picked up the flute in third grade and was a natural. Other nights, Jimm played guitar, I played the flute, and my mom would get silly keeping rhythm with spoons or by banging on a wash tub.

The benefits of living in an inner city in California included a plethora of free after-school or summer activities for children. These were often funded by grants given to the local school systems or parks and recreational services. In addition to the private flute lessons that my grandparents paid for, my mother made sure I was exposed to every activity or class that was offered. I took gymnastics, baton lessons, cooking, sewing, and pottery. We made weekly trips to the public library checking out the current Caldecott and Newbery Award books for children. Our nightly routine was to cuddle up in bed and take turns reading a chapter to each other. Oh, the torrents of tears we cried reading *Charlotte's Web*. On July 17, 1975, I was no longer an only child. My mother delivered a beautiful, very hairy, brown-eyed baby girl and named her Alicia Jean.

My first encounter with conflict was when Jimm's fifteen-year-old brother, Jack, came to California for a visit. One evening, we took a drive in our white hippie van, nicknamed "DORF." Jimm had creatively rearranged the FORD letters on the front of the vehicle. The inside had been renovated with custom beds and cabinets, making it perfect for camping, a homemade mini RV. While my parents toured Jack around Los Angeles, I had fallen asleep in the back of the van. At some point on the drive, Jack moseyed his way to the back, snuggled up beside me, and slid his hand down the front of my panties, exploring parts of my third-grade body no one should be touching. Panic and fear clouded all thought processes. I squeezed my thighs together preventing his perversion, sat up, and moved to the opposite side of the van. I do not recall how quickly I told my mom, but Jack was sent back to Pennsylvania a few days later. I was heard, validated, and safe once again. Nothing more was ever spoken of this incident and my life returned to that of a normal, healthy little girl. *I would later learn through journals of my mother's that Jimm's reaction to this event was "Oh, come on Linda, don't overreact. He is a teenage boy."*

Linda and Christon - Wedding Day

Christon and Alicia

take the money and run

The Steve Miller Band

The summer of 1978 we packed our belongings and caravanned across the country to Panama City, Florida. My grandparents had retired there and Jimm wanted to start his own stereo business and get out of the rat race in Los Angeles. My mother's younger brothers, Tom and Bo, had been living with us in California for a few years training with Jimm in electronics. Although Jimm had no degree or formal training, he was gifted with building and repairing motherboards which were in virtually all stereos, televisions, and soon to be computers. This had been a passion of his since childhood, when he made his first transistor radio.

We traveled with multiple cars, a van, a boat, and a large U-Haul which everyone took shifts driving. At one point, Jimm and I were alone in his canary-yellow 1969 Camaro, when he asked me to steer. I climbed onto his lap, controlling the wheel while he handled the pedals with his feet. Reaching over the gear shift, he opened the glove compartment, retrieving a pipe and small ziplock bag. He opened the bag and took a pinch of what he called "hash," stuffed it into a hole at the top of the pipe, lit it, and inhaled slowly. All while "we" drove on the interstate. No seat belts. No concern of second-hand smoke. No fear of driving under the influence. Cruising across the country on I-10 at 65 mph, getting high while your nine-year-old daughter sits on your lap steering. Sadly, I would be much older before I would realize that this was not normal parenting…not to mention illegal.

The Sound Warehouse was a family owned corporation composed of my parents, Uncle Tom, Uncle Bo, and his wife Tanya. The business opened within a year of our arrival in Panama City. They sold home and auto stereo systems, provided installations, and repaired anything electronic. At some point t-shirts were sold as a form of advertising. I can still visualize one of the shirts in vivid detail. It was a blue t-shirt with black lettering and graphics. In the center of the shirt was a large pile of naked bodies, both men and women, and above it in an arc read "I Got Turned on at The Sound Warehouse."

Money was extremely tight as the business got off its feet, so my parents, sister and I lived in the back of the warehouse for a few months. I vaguely recall stacks of clothes, sleeping pallets on the floor, and boxes everywhere. We heated water on a camping stove for our baths and poured it into a large metal basin. For a child, this was an amazing adventure!

My grandparents and Great-Uncle Don, were often a source of financial support for our family during these years. Uncle Don was my grandfather's baby brother, fourteen years younger, and was living in San Francisco at the time. Due to recurring health issues, my mother encouraged him to move to Florida so he would be closer to family. The house we had rented after getting out of the warehouse was small, forcing Uncle Don to sleep on a cot in our laundry room.

Shortly after my mother delivered a blue-eyed baby boy, who she thoughtfully named Donald, they were able to purchase our first home. It was a spacious two story brick home with a pool located in a great neighborhood and school district. Of course, none of it would have been possible if Uncle Don had not contributed financially.

It did not take long for my mother to pine for the simpler days in California. There she felt understood and only had Jimm and two children to please. The revolving health crisis with her uncle, constant need of approval from her parents, a newborn, and the launching of a business made living in Panama City much more complicated than she had ever envisioned. Her parents'

loose comments about her weight, cigarette addiction, or lack of
professional career added to her insecurity.

My Mother's Journal:
1981 New Year's Resolutions
    1. Do 25 sit-ups per day starting Jan 1st.
    2. Get down to 115 lbs.
    3. Stop smoking.
    4. Increase my creative writing ability-try publishing!
    5. Be a better housekeeper.
    6. Be more patient.
    7. Be a better Christian.
    8. Be a better wife and lover to my dear Jimm.
    9. Learn more about the business.

The educational system in the county was broken down
into four types of schools: elementary schools, sixth grade centers,
middle schools, and high schools. The two sixth grade centers were
ideal for the awkward eleven to twelve year old who was too cool for
elementary school but too immature for middle school. Sixth grade
was my first exposure to changing classes for each subject. My best
friend, Theresa Hawkins, sat beside me in Mr. Sanford's English class.
We thought he was such a cool teacher because he never omitted the
cuss words when he read *The Princess Bride* aloud to our class. This
definitely kept our attention as we giggled silently in our seats. These
were simple days when our biggest responsibility was to make weekly
charts of what we would wear each day so we could twin, or assign
who would be bringing candy on Friday. Theresa's family moved
to Virginia at the end of the school year, but this did not derail our
special friendship. We wrote letters, called each other frequently,
and even visited on summer breaks. *Someone asked me recently if I could
remember the earliest spiritual seed planted in my life and immediately I thought
of the dozens of letters Theresa had written to me, most of them closing with a
Bible verse or simply, "Jesus loves you."*
    School nurses were sent into the classroom a few times that
year. They would separate the boys and the girls for talks about
sex, body image changes, and to administer a scoliosis screening.
These talks heightened my insecurity and self-consciousness because

my body was not changing. Many of my friends had started their menstrual cycles the year prior and had bras the size of my mothers. In order to fit in, I begged for a training bra. I wasn't sure how this small piece of fabric would train my breasts to grow, but I was desperate. It is embarrassing to admit that squeezing my palms together and chanting, "I must, I must, I must increase my bust" was also a daily exercise I thought might help stimulate growth. The first day I wore my new bra, a boy ran up behind me in PE class, grabbed the back strap and popped it like a slingshot, yelling, "Christy is wearing a bra!" I was completely mortified.

The scoliosis screening seemed benign. We were asked to slowly bend down and touch our toes while a nurse stood behind us writing a few notes on a clipboard. As we exited the room, I was the only girl in my class who was handed a letter to take home. This letter notified my parents that I had failed the scoliosis screening and would need to follow up with an orthopedist.

> *My Journal:*
> *Dear Diary,*
> *I have to wear a back brace and it is UGLY! None of my clothes will fit over this gross brace. It isn't fair! I am short, ugly, and have blonde hair that looks awful. I make A's and B's but I don't know how because I am so dumb. I have so many things wrong with me. When I was younger I had to wear braces on my feet because I was pigeon-toed. Now I have to wear this back brace for a year, I need braces on my teeth, a contact for one eye and both my pinky fingers are crooked. I wish I wasn't born. So much money has been spent trying to fix me. My mom says I am lucky because all of these things can be corrected. I surely don't feel lucky. I am only lucky for one reason and that is because I have a great mom and dad! I love them a lot!*
> *Please don't tell anyone what I told you,*
> *Christy*

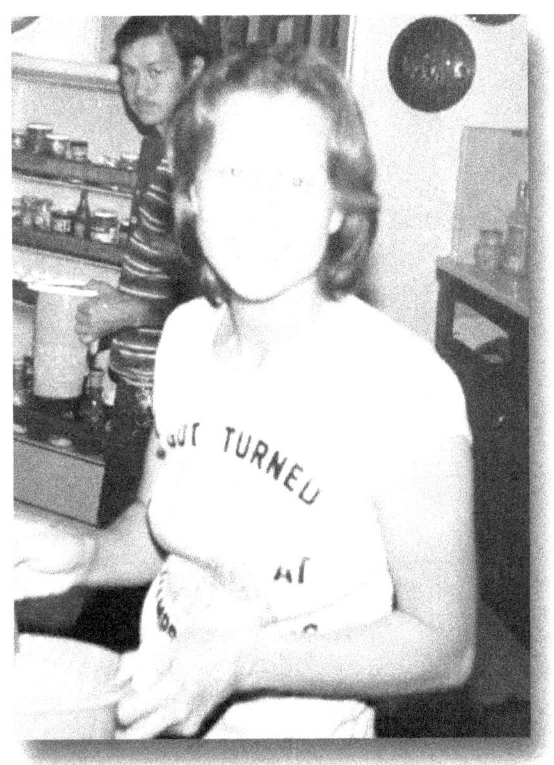

My mother's friend Edwina wearing
I Got Turned on at The Sound Warehouse t-shirt

The Sound Warehouse
with Jimm's '69 Camaro out front [right]

CHAPTER 4
the logical song

Supertramp

Childhood innocence and naivety began to fade as I entered middle school. The reality of my family members' lifestyles became more clear. Uncle Don was a gentle and generous man who sadly battled demons of addiction and depression, admitting himself into the hospital on a regular basis to dry out. I began noticing his intermittent bouts of vigorous tremors at the dinner table where more food would reside on his tailored shirt than would enter his mouth. Weeks would pass with no sign of him. When I questioned his absence, my parent's response was either, "He is sleeping," or, "He is in the hospital." On one occasion, I snuck into his room and found the bathroom counters covered in pill bottles and liquor hidden in odd places.

The most alarming scene was coming home from school to find Uncle Don sitting in his favorite recliner, holding the dog's food bowl. He was eating ice cream that he had scooped on top of moist dog food. When I questioned him, his eyes popped open. They were glazed and began dancing wildly around the room. His speech was slurred and incoherent as he inserted a spoonful of the mixture into his mouth. The alcohol and prescription medications he was consuming regularly were a toxic combination, landing him in the hospital once again.

Years later, I would find his journals, learning many things about my great-uncle that helped to explain his troubled soul. His father, my great-grandfather, was an alcoholic and had abandoned the family shortly after Don's birth. Uncle Don was significantly younger than his two older brothers and they were already out of the house during his teen years. Living with his mother and aunts, he struggled with his masculinity. There were no male influences to teach him how to throw a ball or swing a bat. Instead, he excelled both academically and musically, playing the flute and piano. The bullying and teasing were relentless, causing depression, anxiety, and insecurity to embed into his core. As a young adult, he regularly saw a psychiatrist, having numerous rounds of shock therapy to "reset" his brain. This barbaric treatment was thought to cure people of their homosexual tendencies, depression, and anxiety.

Uncle Don's oldest brother was my grandfather, Thomas, who I called Poppi. I adored him, but he too, struggled with alcohol. I do not know when the drinking began, but it was present when my mother was a teenager. She remembers him coming home from work and pouring a cocktail every night to unwind. As a child, I recall statements like, "Hurry, we need to get over to your grandparents so we can leave by 5pm." This was the "witching hour" when his tongue became loose, rehashing any past mistakes or weaknesses in your life in a sharp demeaning tone. I was the oldest grandchild and we had a very special bond. Thankfully, I never received his tongue lashing, however, my sweet mother was often his primary target. My grandfather, when sober, was a loving man but unfortunately showed it by giving his children money or expensive gifts. His love was performance driven. If they dressed a certain way, donned a tailored haircut, attended college, chose an acceptable major, married the right person, landed a high end job, then his love abounded. Failures were never forgotten and were vented when he consumed alcohol. Needless to say, this caused a tremendous amount of secrecy in our family.

My grandmother, Joan, who I called Gagga, went to great lengths to keep her children's and grandchildren's transgressions hidden from her husband in order to spare them from ridicule. The only time I recall my grandmother keeping a secret about me from

my grandfather was when I double pierced my ears in high school.
I had no idea that his generation considered women promiscuous if
they had ear piercings. This explains the reason my grandmother only
wore clip-on earrings. Gagga was afraid he would be disappointed in
me and asked if I would take them out when he was present. I longed
to please my grandfather and also feared his rebuke, so without
hesitation, I removed the earrings permanently.

My mother's brother Tom was born in Honolulu, Hawaii,
and was seven years younger. When he was in elementary school, he
was diagnosed with a genetic disorder called Muscular Dystrophy.
Despite progressive muscle atrophy, Tom was incredibly intelligent,
played the trumpet, loved acting, and had an amazing speaking voice.
He was handsome and blessed with a plethora of gifts, but had an
unhealthy co-dependency on his parents. Due to guilt that they had
contributed to his disability, his parents overcompensated by funding
him in every way. This handicapped Tom more than his disability
ever did. Therefore, he was irresponsible with even the most basic
of tasks, like taking his daily medications. He also ignored the
consequences of mixing his medications with alcohol or drugs. This
would pose numerous life-threatening situations when diagnosed
with schizophrenia in his twenties.

The baby of the family, Robert, who everyone called Bo,
was thirteen years younger than my mother. He would struggle his
entire life with rebellious entitlement, drugs, and alcohol abuse. My
grandfather, a military man, had certain expectations for his children
and higher education was a must. Bo refused. He would marry three
times, all ending in divorce. In between one of his marriages, he had
a live-in girlfriend named Peggy. Ignoring the red flags and warnings
from friends and family, Bo woke one morning to find Peggy dead
in his living room. The night before they had attended a wild party,
returning home at the break of dawn. While Bo slept, Peggy retrieved
his shotgun, situated the trigger between her toes, and pulled the
trigger. My grandfather and mother would spend two gruesome days
cleaning her blood and brains off the walls, ceiling, and floors of
his home. An autopsy would reveal marijuana, cocaine, and alcohol
in her bloodstream. The destruction of all of Bo's relationships
had one common thread: drugs and alcohol. Unfortunately, Bo was

a user, not only of substances, but of people. Sadly, this included family. It was nauseating to watch him appear on his birthday or at Christmas to receive a check from his father, when there had been no communication from him for months.

I was more observant during these years, taking note of people's body language, tone of voice, or behaviors. At one family gathering, I realized everyone smoked cigarettes except my grandparents. Later, I learned that my grandmother smoked too, she just kept it a secret from my grandfather. She hid cigarettes in a Sucrets cough lozenges box in the back of their bathroom closet. On many occasions, I would count the number of drinks people consumed, curious why some drinks were ingested so much faster than others. I also did not know why some cigarettes were purchased at the store and others were rolled at home. Was this to save money? It would not be long before all of these questions would be answered.

family tradition

Hank Williams, Jr.

Uncle Don and Jimm had a favorite room they called the music room. This room had a top-of-the-line Alpine stereo system and walls lined with albums and cassette tapes. A large bust of Beethoven was displayed on a shelf, with various photographs of musicians hanging on the walls. Rarely were children allowed to enter.

One Friday night in eighth grade, I invited a popular ninth-grade girl to spend the night. I begged my Dad to let us hang out in the room to chill and listen to music. Everything was great until she plucked something out of the ashtray. With a look of excitement, she exclaimed, "Let's smoke this!" I must have looked puzzled because she went on to say, "It's a joint. You know, marijuana? Does your dad smoke these?"

Why was she acting so weird? This was not something exciting or new. My mind was spinning as I thought through what I did know: Jimm grew the plants in the backyard, dried the leaves in his closet, and placed them into a beautifully carved wooden box in the music room. Relaxing in the evenings, listening to music, he would either insert the crushed leaves into a pipe or roll them in small thin pieces of paper to smoke. My friend's excitement and barrage of questions made me realize that this must not be a normal parent pastime. Instantly, I became aware that there was a difference between the store-bought cigarettes and the organic ones grown in our backyard that Jimm dried, rolled, and smoked.

There were many times when I thought my friends liked my parents more than they liked me. They would say things like, "Chris, your parents are so cool, let's hang out at your house."

A battle warred within me as I observed my friends participating in similar activities my parents did at "grown up" parties. As a child, it was so much fun when my parents played loud music, danced, and acted silly when their friends came over. As a teenager it annoyed me because I recognized that their conduct was substance induced. The hours of alcohol and drugs would often lead to misbehavior by the end of the night. For example, insane shaving cream fights would break out both inside and outside the house, leaving me angry when hours of clean up would reveal stains on walls, carpet, or furniture. My mother's response was always, "Oh Twink, it's just stuff."

On several occasions, the police were called for loud music or disorderly conduct. The worst incident was when a police helicopter landed on our street. Yep, right in front of our house! The helicopter was flying over our home and someone at the party had the brilliant idea to grab a flood light and point it directly at the helicopter. I do not remember specifically what the policeman in the helicopter said over the speaker, but he was very angry. Jimm was almost arrested that evening and I was terrified. *Thirty years later, Jimm would say to me, "Chris, you were the adult in our family, you kept your mom and I in line."*

The first time I recall being asked to keep a secret about my parents' recreational activities occurred one evening after a flute lesson. I came home to find my favorite teacher hanging out with Jimm in the music room. At first, I was nervous that maybe I had failed a math test and he had set up a conference with my parents. However, within seconds I noticed a familiar smell. The red-stained eyes and delayed body movements gave it all away. Family, friends, and now teachers all participating in mind altering activities left me feeling confused and alone.

My family did not attend church, so when a friend invited me to attend a tent revival I was indifferent, but agreed to go.

Hundreds of people sat outside under a large white tent while a loud charismatic man talked about Jesus from a platform. When he was done, a band began to play music. The crowd sang along, raising their hands with their eyes closed. There was a weird butterfly feeling inside of me that I did not understand. At the end of one of the songs, a gentleman grabbed the microphone and said, "There is someone in this room that feels confused and alone. She wants to be different, but is surrounded by people who are leading her down the wrong road. If that is you, please come up here. We want to pray with you." It felt like he was talking directly to me. Without hesitation, my heart beating out of my chest, I walked to the front.

People were kneeling at numerous wooden structures, resembling small two-foot-high balance beams, scattered in front of the stage. Clueless, I knelt at one when out of nowhere hands were on my head and I heard men talking in a strange language. Attempting to look up, a hand pushed my head back down. The peaceful butterfly feeling was now replaced with fear. As tears streamed down my face, I was assisted to a standing position where I was encouraged to stand on the balance beam. There were three men, one on my left and another on my right, holding my hands to steady me as I walked across the wooden beam. The third man repeated, "Say you love Jesus." When I quietly obeyed, he whispered, "Say it louder." At that moment, I would have done a backflip on the beam if it meant getting away from these crazy people. Once back in my seat, I vowed to stay far away from churches, especially ones in tents.

The Music Room

its too late

Carole King

Over the next few years our immediate family would be shaken like an unexpected California earthquake. I had always felt safe and secure with my parents, never questioning their love. Little did I know that Jimm, the only seemingly stable man in my life, was standing on a precipice of self-destruction. Unfortunately, his deceit and self-centeredness would not only destroy our family, but it would leave deep scars in each of us for life.

As business picked up, the mounting workload forced Jimm to spend long hours at work, causing my mom to feel lonely and insecure. The stress mixed with many dysfunctional family relationships became a toxic mix in their marriage.

Excerpt from letter:
To: Jimm
From: Linda
1983
May start rambling, but this is all "off the top" yet, at the same time, guttural. First of all, I love you, and want to stay with you, forever and ever, amen! Strangely, I was surviving reasonably well when we first met. I seemed to have all those wonderful assets; charm, intelligence, wit, beauty, self-confidence, and respect. I became "blinded by love" because nothing else mattered as long as we were together. I felt safe,

secure and especially totally loved!

The children, responsibilities and our business are all growing. Yet, our oneness has drifted into two. I have become a parasite that depends on you to nourish my soul. I am definitely the weaker, finding myself unable to stand strong alone. I have lost myself!

Maybe it is because you are a futurist, thinking about the tomorrows and I am a now-ist, thinking about the moment. Unfortunately, your future and my present very seldom intermingle. I have become too dependent after nine years with you. I don't expect you to change, you are happy and content with yourself, it is Linda who is not. Guess I'd like you to be a part of everything I do, and visa-versa. However, it has reached a point where basic communication is impossible.

Why is searching for a life on my own so difficult? This is not what I had envisioned. There are just so many contradictions: you celebrate with others but not with me, you can stay up all night on a project but can't find the time for us. I would gladly sit there and talk with you while you worked or assist you if I could be included. Our paths occasionally crossing are not filling the void.

For years, we have done everything as a team. Building our life together, building a business and growing our family. Now, I feel like a surrogate, my job is done and I am no longer needed. I don't fit in with the people in this town. Always felt like you were the only one who truly understood me. Now, I am faced with the realization that you were only "tolerating" me. How miserably alone I am!

There also was growing tension at The Sound Warehouse. Bo and his wife Tanya divorced after he found her in bed with his best friend on his lunch break. In stubborn pride neither of them left their positions at the business. Awkwardness mounted as they both remarried within a year. Explosive arguments were becoming a daily affair between Bo and Jimm. Much of it, we thought, was brought on by Bo's poor work ethic and increased drug use. A few of Jimm's closest confidants began secretly relaying information that my mother had feared all along.

My Mother's Journal:

July 1984

The last few days, Jimm has gone into work with a miserable attitude. Pure hatred dripping from his mouth in regards to my brother Bo. I suggested he call a quick corporate meeting to vote Bo out of the business but he lashed back with, "A conversation won't help. I want revenge!"

Something felt off this morning when Jimm left unusually early for work. These feelings were validated when I received a phone call around 9:30 am from Carrie (Bo's second wife). She frantically explained that Jimm intentionally came in early to ambush Bo. He had turned the circuit breaker off and was hiding in the dark when Bo unlocked the shop. As Bo was stumbling to find the circuit breaker, arms full with donuts and coffee, Jimm jumped out and attacked Bo without warning.

*My first reaction was to call or drive up to The Sound Warehouse to get more details but instead decided to let things marinate. Upon returning home from running a few errands, I found out that Jimm had been home briefly to take a quick shower. He told Chris that he had succeeded in beating the sh** out of her uncle, and if Bo ever returned to work he will do it again. I am disgusted, repulsed and totally confused. I've never seen uncontrollable violence in Jimm and it makes me ill. This is NOT my husband!*

My Mother's Journal:

August 1984

I was told that a large shipment came in on Thursday in which Jimm and Bo were to split. Jimm was unaware that it had arrived and that Bo had sold all of it. Jimm was livid, revenge and retaliation were in his soul. When I questioned Jimm, he admitted to the shipment and that he was to receive half, however, refused to admit that this was the reason for his escalating anger toward my brother by stating, "I've carried his butt for years and talking is no longer possible."

I have assumed for years that this "shipment" was cocaine. One, because a few months prior to this entry my mom writes about confronting Bo's second wife, Carrie, on rumors of their frequent cocaine use. Second, three months after this fight, she writes of another person who had come forward with information about Jimm's erratic behavior.

> *My Mother's Journal:*
> *Mr. Smitty called today stating that he saw Jimm at Waffle House at 4 am. Jimm was drunk and bragging about a chick he had met at the bar, Montego Bay. Funny, Jimm told me he had driven to Tyndall Beach and sat there for hours all alone. Mr. Smitty also relayed that a very large shipment came in last night. This entire thing is finally getting completely out of control.*

CHAPTER 7

Gloria Gaynor

My mother found a small Methodist church near our home and met with the pastor, Kenneth Taylor, for marital counseling. This church had no white tents, the pastor did not yell, and if you needed to pray at the front of the church, no one attacked you.

Our immediate family and grandmother, Gagga, would attend this church periodically over the next few years. My siblings and I were baptized by sprinkling, even though none of us were aware of its symbolic meaning. Attending church together would be short-lived, but the memories that are kindled make me smile. Superfluous things like all of us dressing up, the endless disbursement of candy from Gagga's purse to keep us occupied, the jingle of my mother's bracelets when she moved, and the sweet smell of my grandmother's perfume. Then there was the silent giggling when the handful of elderly sang off-key from a musty hardback book, which I would later learn was called a hymnal.

Up to this point in my life, I don't recall God ever being a topic of conversation. If a prayer was ever uttered it was rote, like the one occasionally said at Thanksgiving: *God is great, God is good, let us thank Him for our food. By His hands we are fed. Give us Lord our daily bread, Amen.* Or the one memorized to say at bedtime which instilled a little fear: *Now I lay me down to sleep, I pray to the Lord my soul to keep. If I should die before I wake, I pray the Lord my soul to take, Amen.* I don't remember any sermons or specific Bible verses used during my introduction to church, but a complete awareness of a spiritual world with a God who is much bigger than my parents was emblazoned on my heart.

During one of my parents' counseling sessions, Jimm shared a dark time in his life while living in Los Angeles. He attended church with a friend and unbeknownst to him, it was satanic. Over the years, I have forgotten all the creepy details of the ways the members relentlessly pursued him and the fear they wielded to coerce him into their cult. Pastor Taylor asked if he would share this experience with the churches youth group.

Arrangements were made to record the event for those who could not attend. The equipment was assembled with a last minute sound check, "Testing, testing, 1-2-3." Everything was ready, the room was filled with teenagers, and the button was pressed to record his testimony. At the end, Jimm answered questions from the audience about his ordeal.

The following day, Jimm received a frantic call from the pastor asking to meet him in his office immediately after work. When he arrived, the pastor pressed play on his stereo system and the two men sat stunned as they listened to the tape from the previous evening. "Testing, testing, 1-2-3," was heard followed, by the pastor introducing Jimm. No words are heard from Jimm again. You hear rustling of feet, movements, whispers and all other voices in the room except Jimm's. His voice was gone.

Fifteen years later, my mother was hospitalized for severe abdominal pain. Her appendix, a portion of her intestines and a benign tumor the size of an orange were all removed. As I sat with her in the hospital, a gentleman entered the room that I vaguely recognized. Pastor Taylor saw my mother's name on the board at the nurses' station and dropped in to check on her. After a sweet reunion and prayer, he left with me following closely behind. I needed a moment with him. What were his memories of my parents? Did he recall the strange events the night Jimm spoke to the youth group? To my surprise, he said "I had always believed in spiritual warfare, but that night it became real! I saw it, I heard it, and my life has never been the same."

By the end of ninth grade, my parents' relationship
was spiraling out of control and I had become a pawn in their
dysfunctional relationship. My mother was heartbroken and desperate
to try anything to restore their marriage, often confiding her pain to
me in vivid details. Jimm, on the other hand, was aloof and distant
when it came to their marriage. Riding with him on business errands,
he would flirt inappropriately with women while I watched from the
Camaro. Pain, confusion, and anger would well up inside me, only
to be suppressed, fearing the revelations would devastate my sweet
mother. *I was unaware that my mother knew of Jimm's infidelity until I read
her journals years after her death.*

> *My Mother's Journal:*
> *August 1984*
> *I've always been made out to be so stupid, so idiotic-and
> so guilty for being open about my uncomfortable feelings
> towards (she lists six separate women) and now numerous
> friends of yours have come forward confirming my
> uneasiness. "Oh, you didn't know Linda? I have seen Jimm
> at the beach on numerous occasions with a woman in his
> car." I had often stated in my younger, more naïve days,
> that if a man was to ever hit me or had any type of sexual
> relations with another woman, I would be gone! Strangely, I
> would be able to forgive it all if only I had love, honesty, and
> most importantly, verbal and physical communication. I am
> writing this in an attempt to figure out all that has occurred.
> To correct, alleviate, and change things in my personality in
> order to make our relationship indestructible. If all of these
> affairs have indeed existed or still exist, then there MUST be
> something amiss with me, BIGTIME!*
>
> *We went for a drive tonight to talk and felt optimistic
> that we would reconcile. However, I was sadly disappointed.
> As I expressed my love for him, sharing that I would give up
> my right arm or one of my breasts to keep him, he told me
> he had no love left for me. My touch did nothing for him,
> his heart was gone, and that he found himself happier away
> from me.*

One night, while I was sleeping, my door opened and a night light from the hallway bathroom cast a shadow over an adult male figure that was slowly walking towards my bed. Questions raced through my mind: *What time is it? Who is that? Why are they in my room?* Still groggy from sleep, I lay still, not sure if I was dreaming. The male slowly slid his hand under my covers, finding the waistband to my panties. Fear suffocated me. His hand continued down the front of my panties, touching me. I could not speak but quickly squeezed my legs together, rolling over close to the wall. This startled the male, causing him to abruptly withdraw his hand and gently pull the covers up as if he were tucking me into bed. That's when I heard Jimm speak, "Shhh Twink, you must be having a bad dream." With those words, he slowly left, closing my bedroom door. I lay in bed paralyzed, nauseated by the reality of who had just touched me. This incident felt too familiar.

For weeks, I shuffled through school and activities in a stupor, locking my bedroom door at night. The emotional turmoil and secrecy raging within led to physical ailments that kept me home from school for days at a time.

> *My Mother's Journal:*
> *Took Chris to the doctor today, stomach spasms of some type. The blood work and urinalysis were normal. She has been out of school all week, sleeping most of the time.*

The unusual distancing and unexplained health problems concerned my mother. She was alarmed to find my door locked when coming to say good night one evening. When I opened the door, her beautiful blue eyes revealed an immediate awareness of my pain. The days and weeks I spent hiding, frantically building a fortress around my pain, disintegrated the moment our eyes met, revealing my secret. In an instant our brokenness collided into a torrent of tears. I felt safe, certain that she would handle the situation just like she had when Jimm's brother had touched me in the third grade.

That evening when Jimm strolled in late from work, she immediately confronted him. He vehemently denied the accusation, stating, "I went to tuck her in and she was having a bad dream."

The next morning there was a letter poking out of the front pocket of my book bag. In the letter, Jimm expressed his deep love for me, claiming he would never do anything to hurt me or my siblings. He blamed my "bad dream" on the months of stress our family was experiencing. Unfortunately, my mother believed him. Once again, I stuffed the pain, trying to convince myself that our family's current circumstances were indeed a very bad dream.

As I looked around for a stable adult in my life, there was none to be found. So I began experimenting with alcohol and marijuana. Why not, this is how the adults coped.

all out of love

Air Supply

The first semester of high school, my parents officially separated and Jimm moved out of our home. My mother was made out to be the bad guy as he took every opportunity to tell friends and customers that she had kicked him out.

> *My Mother's Journal:*
> *Jimm is existing well on the "poor Jimm syndrome." He tells people, "I only have cold water at The Sound Warehouse, no hot meals, Linda won't let me see the children, and all I do is work." These lies are making it difficult to manage emotionally and physically. My heart feels dead. Chris is full of hatred for Jimm, Alicia has some strange form of hope, and Donnie seems unaffected. Donnie did ask Jimm on Sunday, "When will you be back, Daddy?" Jimm replied, "As soon as possible!" There are so many mixed messages. He tells something different to each person.*

Days later, my nine-year-old sister Alicia would find Uncle Don dead in his bedroom. Autopsy revealed that the cause of death was a heart arrhythmia at the age of fifty-two. My mother was devastated. She was convinced that the stress of Jimm moving out was too much for Uncle Don and he was beginning to see the destruction Jimm was causing in everyone's lives. This would be the first loved one in my life to pass away and I did not know how to process the pain. I had tremendous guilt that I had not loved and respected Uncle Don like I should have. I wrote the following letter shortly after his death, trying to sort out my emotions and guilt.

> *To: Uncle Don*
> *From: Chris*
> *How are you? Where are you? Are you ok? I just wanted to write and check on you. I want you to know that I learned a lot from you. I promise not to say my name first anymore (she and I). The only reason I play my flute now is for you. Every time you hear me playing I hope it makes you smile. You NEVER had to buy my love, you ALWAYS had it! I know at times I didn't show it but I am just a kid. I miss you and I want you back! But since I can't have you back, will you please send me your strength and your love? Why did you leave us? Come home PLEASE!!!!*
> *Love your niece, Chris*

Panama City was a small town and Jimm was connected to so many influential people. Most of the local restaurants, bars, and businesses had purchased stereo equipment from The Sound Warehouse. He also provided the sound for beauty pageants and performances at the Marina Civic Center. Even the teenagers loved Jimm. The weekend hotspot for teens was the beach, so having sweet sounding tunes booming from your speakers was important for flirting and cruising down The Strip. Many of these teens had spent countless paychecks and hours at The Sound Warehouse. Jimms' diversity in music genres and expertise in the business made him a cult hero.

Few knew the truth about my home life and it was getting exceedingly harder to keep it a secret. Especially when so many people were spotting Jimm in shady places with inappropriate people. Not to mention, he was openly discussing his failing marriage with my classmates inside and outside of the shop.

As the rumors escalated, I could no longer defend Jimm or

rationalize his behaviors. The things he said no longer aligned with his actions. I was now driving and desperate for the truth. It wasn't difficult to spot a bright yellow Camaro, but my stalking came with a cost. I naively thought that if I knew the truth it would bring freedom from all the lies. However, the things I saw engulfed me in a deep chasm of pain and even more confusion.

Oddly, the little girl in me still wanted to please her daddy and have a relationship with him while the maturing teen hated his guts. This ambivalence towards Jimm was seen in the following letter that I left on the windshield of his Camaro.

To: Jimm
From: Chris
Dad,
I realize that you have a lot to worry about. It is very easy to see that you are only concerned with my siblings, not me. Here are a few examples:

1. *You invite Alicia and Donnie to dinner, to hang out or spend the night. I never get an invitation.*
2. *When you drop them off you don't even come to the door to say "hello" to me.*

Please, don't give me any crap about how I could come outside and say "hello" to you. I am sick and tired of kissing your butt. You are supposed to be such a great father but I sure don't see any greatness. You show no love towards me at all. It is obvious that you could care less if I even existed. As far as I can see, it is only Alicia and Donnie that matter to you.
Thanks for your time, Chris

My Mother's Journal:
*When Jimm and I spoke today he said, "Linda, you are depressing to be around. I find more pleasure in being around other people. Look, as far as the kids go, all I want is Donnie. You can take Alicia and then Chris can do whatever the **** she wants to!" From this conversation one can only assume that our relationship has been terminated.*

My mother's pendulum of emotions clouded her ability to think rationally. This was a heartbreaking reality. One day she would curse the ground Jimm walked on, determined to move on without him. The following day she would cry and pine for restoration in their marriage. Secretly, my hatred for him mounted as I helplessly watched this beautiful woman crumble. I wanted to scream, "Pull yourself together, he isn't worth it!"

On November 10, 1984, I arrived home to an empty house. My sister and brother were staying the night with friends and my mother was gone. There was a weird sinking feeling in the pit of my stomach as I entered the kitchen. Laying on the counter was a note written by my mother. Normally she had impeccable handwriting, but the scribble on this page was almost illegible.

> *To: Chris, Alicia and Donnie*
> *From: Mom*
> *10 November 1984*
> *Another lousy weekend! Wish I could be strong, but I'm not. I am weak and the weak don't survive, as we all know. The only solution that I can see is to end it all.*
>
> *Chris, you are so talented and beautiful. I love you, please try to understand. All I have ever wanted was for someone to really love and take care of me. To be my friend and my lover. I can't wait any longer for things to turn around. I'm worried quite frankly about Alicia, my little brown eyed beauty. She needs a lot of love. Please help her understand that I am not deserting her. Be strong girls, you both have so much to offer this world.*

Frantically, I called my grandparents. Friends and family searched every bar and hotel from Panama City Beach to Mexico Beach for two days. Unfortunately, there were no cell phones or Life 360 in 1984. Forty-eight hours later, Uncle Bo found her in a dumpy hotel. She was emotionally drained, dehydrated, and hung over, but she was ALIVE. There would never be a single word or whisper about this event again. As a matter of fact, if I had not found the suicide letter folded in her journal thirty-four years later, I may not have recalled a single thing. The moment I unfolded it and saw the writing I was overwhelmed with emotions. My hands shook just like they did all those years ago, as I recalled the fear of never seeing her again. Even after ruminating on those horrible memories, I remember absolutely nothing about the two days she was missing. My mind is a blank slate. Did we stay at home alone or go to relatives? Are those memories blocked because the fear, stress, and grief was too much for a sixteen-year-old to bear? Evidently, my mother wrote another note to us during her meltdown. This one I had never seen before and was written on elementary school paper one day later. The penmanship was beautiful with no errors or smudges.

> *To: Chris, Alicia, and Donnie*
> *From: Mom*
> *11 November 1984*
> *There is so much I want to relay to all three of you, but so little time now. I love you more than anything or anyone. You are the best! Everyone has faults and mine is that I am not a fighter, I'm a quitter. I can't go on! You will be stronger without me, believe me!*
>
> *Love is a funny thing, or should I say a strange thing. I love your Dad, but for some reason I am unable to express it properly. Remember to always communicate with your spouse. Never let talking to one another dwindle, even with your siblings. Keep your relationship alive! Every relationship in my life has disappeared and dissolved. I have no one. Life is extremely short, enjoy every minute and make the most out of your life. I have accomplished nothing. I am a failure and can not support myself or any of you.*
>
> *Please, all of you, go places, do things, and don't let anyone stop you from becoming a self-supporting individual. Try also to understand that I love you! I know it is hard, but please try and understand! Get along with one another and be happy. I'm not, but it has nothing to do with any of you. I've been fortunate to have three loving and caring children. Thank you for giving me this enjoyment, because you three have been my life!*

As the year progressed, I became more and more disconnected. I avoided family functions, dropped out of band, quit dance, and stopped doing school work. Instead, I got a job at a clothing store in the mall and spent time partying with older high school students.

> *My Mother's Journal:*
> *I must talk to Alicia. The last week or so she has been*
> *extremely sensitive. The slightest touch, tease, or reprimand*
> *by friends or family causes tears, fussing, or arguments. I*
> *thought initially it was Jimm's departure, but have suddenly*
> *come to realize that it was my crumbling and taking off for*
> *two nights that is distressing her. She has been even more*
> *protective of me, asking me where I am going, how long I*
> *will be gone, and if I am picking her up after school. Good*
> *grief, she is afraid that I will leave her again. I should*
> *never have left or never have come back! I must get her*
> *to express her feelings, letting it all out. This is of utmost*
> *importance to me right now, nothing else matters. I cannot*
> *continue to hope or want the family to understand me. I must*
> *start understanding them and keep on top of the signs of*
> *insecurities.*

As my mother focused on Alicia, my life continued on a downward spiral. A miserable break up with a boy and a failing English grade was the last straw. Dealing with immense self-loathing, guilt, and my family's dysfunctional state could have been a disastrous combination. Yet, somehow, I knew a reset button was desperately necessary in my life. I unloaded everything in a letter to my mother.

> *Excerpt from letter:*
> *To: Mom*
> *From: Chris*
> *There is definitely a missing link in our relationship right*
> *now. I am always behind you trying to understand you*
> *and soothe you emotionally. I realize that you have a lot*
> *of problems right now with Uncle Don's recent death and*
> *all the crap with Dad. You are so involved with your own*
> *problems and all of Mrs. Dee's (this was one of her best*
> *friends). When I try to talk to you about what I am going*
> *through, you are either too busy or blind. Tonight, you totally*
> *shrugged me off when I tried to tell you some good news.*

You are totally unaware that I have made a lot of mistakes lately. I don't like who I am becoming and I have no one to talk to about it. You are all I have, Mom. If you don't wake up, you might lose me. I have to be honest, tonight I wanted to grab the car keys, leave, and never come back. Please try and understand that you are not the only one hurting.

With everything that has gone on the last few months, I have lost myself. I know this sounds totally crazy, but I want to go to a different high school. I have to get away from some of these people. Oh, and have I told you how much I hate being in the marching band? Please listen to me and help me!

I love you Mommy, Twinkie

I had no idea how my mother would finagle a school transfer within the county, but what I did know was that I did not want to end up like my dysfunctional, addicted family members. The life I had been living over the past school year was aligning me on that same family tree.

Many friends and family members thought my mother was crazy to let a teenager call the shots. They would say, "You are teaching her to be a runner, she needs to suck it up. Confronting conflict will make her stronger." Despite the negativity surrounding my transfer to the rival high school, neither of us swayed from what our hearts knew was a wise decision.

The new high school was a thirty-minute drive from our home. When Uncle Don died, my mom traded in his car and bought me a used candy-apple-red Ford Ranger truck to get back and forth to school and work. The freedom of starting a new life across town gave me a completely different perspective on friends, family, and my future, prompting me to ask myself some tough questions. Did my current friends make me a better person? Did my family really know what was best for me? What kind of a woman did I want to become? This bold move was a choice I had made and it was up to me to prove to everyone that I would succeed.

Christon - 16 years old

Christon's 1st car - Ford Ranger

find a way

Amy Grant

My Mother's Journal:
"For what it's worth, you are the best woman I've ever met,"
was the last statement Jimm made Wednesday night as he
pulled out of the driveway. My comment was "I know, but
it has taken me a long time to realize it." I am definitely
beginning to regain some self-confidence. I will not allow
myself to become insecure again.

I began seeing glimpses of hope, confidence, and joy return to my mother as she trudged through her grief. A good diversion for her was investing in friendships with other women. One of our neighbors, Mrs. Dee, was my mother's closest confidant. Her youngest daughter and my sister, Alicia, were best friends. Watching the little girls swim in the pool, Mrs. Dee and my mother casually sipped on beer as they discussed their failing marriages and parental tips. Unfortunately, Mrs. Dee was an alcoholic and had received one too many DUI's. She was sentenced to an inpatient rehabilitation program for a few months. My mother did all she could to support Mrs. Dee's family, like preparing meals, watching her children, and most importantly, sending letters of encouragement every single day. She saw potential in people, even if they couldn't see it in themselves.

Her hope was to bring their talents to the surface, burying the demons and handicaps holding them back. One of my mother's favorite sayings was, "Tomorrow is a new day." What a gift she had to love people unconditionally. The letters she wrote to her friend proved to be therapy for my mother and a way to document the final year of her marriage.

> *Excerpt from letter:*
> *To: Mrs. Dee*
> *From: Linda*
> *10 January 1985*
> *I find it absolutely disgusting that they would place you in a facility with hardened criminals. Please remember who you are, what's important, and how much you are loved. You are NOT dirty or filthy, don't let those around you rub off on your personality. Keep it together, we have too many things to accomplish. Happiness and contentment are in store for us if we can just survive a few more months. We have too much to offer. The tables will turn.*
>
> *Remember that you are a good person, please don't let this miserable experience defeat you. You are needed, cared about, and most importantly, you are loved. Hang in there sweet lady, you are half-way to your release date. Then watch out world, as a team, we will overcome all of our obstacles. Nothing will slow us down!*

Our strengths can also become our greatest weaknesses. This was certainly the case with my mother. She trusted people to a fault, even if it caused her personal pain or hardship. Although her intentions were genuine, she was easy prey for takers. My mother always saw the good in people, unaware that they were sucking the life, joy, and even money from her without batting an eye. When it came to others, she never gave up on them, saying, "Maybe this time things will be different. If not, my love will fix them." Over the years I watched her attempt this with two husbands, numerous friends, an uncle, her father, both brothers, a boyfriend, and her only son.

My mother had no problem defending others, but when it came to defending herself, she crumbled. In her world, love conquered all, and if it didn't, then she ran to hide. Arguments or unkind words were taken personally and would derail her for days. This forced me to step in and be the peacemaker, always helping her resolve conflict. It became difficult when she was asking me to have more and more interaction with a man I internally despised.

On August 12, 1985, a few days before starting my Junior year at Mosley High School, the divorce was finalized. The emotional wounds and feelings of rejection were at an all-time high. These would need to be suppressed for now, in order to survive and make healthy friendships on new turf.

The first day on campus as I registered for classes, I met three girls who were also new to the high school. We clicked immediately even though our interests were different: Karen was a dancer, Michelle was a cheerleader, Kristen had a beautiful singing voice, and I played the flute. As I sought to excel academically and make a new life for myself, weekends were a struggle. I didn't know the girls well enough to hang out with them on a regular basis after school, and certainly didn't want them to meet my dysfunctional family, so I lived a double life. At school, I pretended to have it all together, never giving away clues that my home life was no longer a safe place for me. On the weekends, I either worked or partied with old friends, the ones I desperately wanted to unplug from my life.

When I did hang out at my new friends' homes, it was drastically different than my own. It wasn't that their parents were married, or houses were bigger or cleaner, it was something deeper. Here are a few specific details I remember: Their homes were organized and had soft pastel hues throughout. My home was cluttered and disorganized with a hippie décor in shades of burnt orange, greens, and browns. Their homes had books on shelves, but the ones that stuck out to me were the worn out Bibles and devotionals in various places, some with a notebook and pen tucked inside. My home had books from all genres, like Helter Skelter: the true story of the Manson Murders, The Joy of Sex, or the Encyclopedia of Macramé. The grotesque pictures in some of these, like Helter Skelter, gave me nightmares for years. I would hide these books behind others on the shelf so I wouldn't have to see them when I walked into the room. We had eclectic art on the walls like pictures of the Beatles or temple rubbings from Japan. My friends' homes had framed family photos, along with beautiful Bible verses displayed in prominent places. There was nothing wrong with my mother's taste in decorating or choice in reading materials. Something was just missing and I could not put my finger on it.

Many of the students at Mosley attended the First Baptist Church downtown. The church offered many activities throughout the week for young people. Sunday night was a church supper followed by youth choir and orchestra practice. On Wednesday nights, teens would gather for music, skits, games, and a message from the youth pastor, Charles Boyd. The students called him Poker, and he was different from any adult male I had ever met. He was humble, genuine, and honest even about his own personal failures. In the beginning, I had a few shallow reasons for attending this church: cute boys, good food, and time away from home. But as I returned every week, there was an undeniable stirring or awakening occurring inside of me.

My Journal:
Went to work immediately after school on Friday. When I got home at nine-thirty, my mother was casually leaning against a car I didn't recognize in the driveway. As I got out of my truck and walked closer, I heard flirtatious laughter and slurred speech. The man with her was Marty. He was one of Uncle Bo's friends that I had met at a family cookout. It was obvious that they had been drinking and were enjoying close

personal contact. I went inside, made a few phone calls, packed a bag and told my mom that I had been invited to stay the night with a friend. It made me sick to see the gleam in her eye at the thought of me leaving and the permission it gave her to be naughty.

I met up with a group of girls and rode out to the beach, wanting to completely forget what I had seen and felt. After a few drinks and drags on a joint, I literally remember nothing. I woke up Saturday morning in a strange bed. My head felt like a sledge hammer breaking up chunks of concrete. I was so confused. Where was I? My eyes slowly came into focus and I could see a few of the girls sprawled out on the floor. As if attempting to walk with a pounding headache wasn't enough, the vision I saw in the mirror was horrifying! Black mascara was smeared down my cheeks and something foul was matted in my hair. Whose clothes was I wearing? I couldn't read the letters on my shirt in the mirror so I looked down…First Baptist Church Softball was printed on the front. Let the vomiting begin!

One of the girls had an uncle who was out of town and she had a key to his apartment. When it was obvious that she could not bring a group of drunk girls home to her mother, she drove us to his place. I was later told that on the way to his apartment, I had vomited on my shirt, and had thrown it out the window. Embarrassed that I had no shirt on, I ran from the car to what I thought was her uncle's apartment. A topless drunk teenager was greeted by a sweet Christian couple who invited me into their apartment at three in the morning. Even though I had interrupted their peaceful sleep, they offered me a glass of water and a new shirt. My girlfriends were mortified, apologizing repeatedly, and escorting me out quickly. Once inside the correct apartment, I was tucked into bed.

I remember nothing! The guilt, shame, embarrassment, and fear of what I did, mixed with all the "what ifs" left me sick as a dog the entire weekend. I promise, I will NEVER do anything like this again!

I went to youth group on Wednesday following this journal entry. When I walked in, Poker asked if I could chat for a few minutes after the service. My heart sank. *Did he know? Did someone tell him where I had been last weekend and the things I had done?* None of my old friends from the other side of town attended church. Surely I was freaking out for no reason. *How had my two worlds collided?* I felt exposed and vulnerable.

Poker and I talked for hours beside my truck in the church parking lot that evening. He began by asking superficial questions that were easy to answer about school, interests and friends. Then he dove deeper into family dynamics and my relationship with God. It was obvious that he cared about the condition of my heart, which made me trust him. For the last few years my mother's dissolving marriage, distressing financial issues, and unstable emotional state were the focus. No one seemed to care or even ask how I was coping. His questions caused me to process and evaluate gaping wounds I had kept hidden from the world. The last thing he said to me that evening was, "Chris, there is an empty place in your heart that only God can fill. The world wants you to shove temporary things into it like drugs, alcohol, sex, money, and even people. All of these things will eventually disappoint you and will never satisfy the void you feel. In spite of your broken places and the things you have done wrong, God loves you and sent his son Jesus to die for you. You can be different." *Oh, if he only knew.*

That night, alone in my room, I asked God to forgive me for all the ways I had messed up. I prayed that He would give me a new life. A life that pleased Him. "Please God," I begged, "help me to be different."

The following Sunday, at the end of the church service, while the choir sang *I Have Decided*, I walked alone to the front of the church. I told the pastor that I had asked Jesus into my heart and

wanted to get baptized. When the music stopped, the pastor shared with the congregation the decision I had made. Although I was all alone, no family to smile at me from the pews, I felt whole for the first time in my life. My circumstances at home were still the same, but I was different.

Writing has been a total act of obedience. Honestly, some days have been torture. However, the closer I got to this chapter the more freedom I felt. The feeling was much like reading the Bible through for the first time, by Malachi, you are desperate for a Savior. I did not know much about the Bible when I asked Jesus into my heart, but what I did know changed everything! If God could take the death of His only son and turn it into something good, then God could take my dysfunctional life and create something beautiful.

i'm not alone

Russ Taff

There were so many things to look forward to as I entered my senior year. I made drum major for the high school marching band, I had a new friend group, I loved my job in the mall, and most importantly, I had a new identity in Jesus. God was slowly super-gluing me back together. *As "adult -me" reflects back to 1986-1987, I am so thankful that God showed up when he did, not sure "teenage-me" could have survived the fallout to come without having the God of the universe to cling to.*

I can't lie, every day was a struggle to stay in my lane, the influences of Hell were in my face at every turn. A girl I had known for years, from my old high school, was forced by her parents to transfer to Mosley. To save on gas, we car-pooled a few days a week. Huge mistake! A new school did nothing to change the types of people she was drawn to or the social life she enjoyed. The biggest pothead at the school, and rumored drug dealer, quickly became her new boyfriend. Many morning rides she would light up a joint on the way to school to "calm her nerves" or "help her focus for a test." We had the same first period class and I am convinced that our teacher smelled the lingering aroma of marijuana on us as we entered the classroom.

The new normal at home was not getting any easier either.

Jimm lived in a trailer he had moved behind The Sound Warehouse and shared custody of my siblings with my mother. The tension between them was unbearable. Some of this was brought on by my mother's new live-in boyfriend, Marty. Her insecurities and desperate need for love and approval brought her into yet another unhealthy relationship.

In the beginning, she tried to keep the relationship and his living arrangements a secret from her parents, knowing they would not approve. Marty would not have been any parent's top pick for a mate. First, he had a criminal record which included multiple DUI's and battery charges. Second, he did not have a college degree or even consistent employment. I vaguely remember his absence for a few days at a time, when he had a temporary job on a shrimping boat. Third, he did not own a home, or even a car, for that matter. The majority of his time was spent at our house, eating our food, smoking, drinking, and sleeping in my mother's bed. He was just another person for my mother to support. The most disturbing to me was his alcohol intake and the influence it was having on my mother. Drinking became a daily habit, and excessive consumption was a guaranteed event on the weekends. All in all he was a likable fella when he was sober. He made my mother feel beautiful, intelligent, and loved until the moment alcohol touched his lips. The alcohol exposed a jealous, controlling man with anger management issues. Their relationship became increasingly toxic; each week was spent drinking, fighting, and making up.

A few years prior, I was given my own phone line in my bedroom. This proved to be a saving grace for our family during the tumultuous courtship between my mother and Marty. Many nights, when the fighting began to escalate, I would quietly wake up my brother and sister, sneak them into my room, lock the door, and call 911. The three of us would snuggle on my twin bed until the police arrived. It didn't take long for Marty to figure out that it was me calling the police. Unnecessary money was being spent on replacing doors, patching walls, and calling the telephone repairman to fix destroyed phone jacks, mine in particular. The silverware drawer even had to be replaced after a drunken tantrum led him to sling the drawer against the wall, sending spoons and forks flying across the kitchen. I found this letter that I had written to God in one of my mother's journals.

To: God
From: Chris
Behind Locked Doors,
Who do I turn to? Who will listen and understand? It is so strange getting older. When I was young I accepted things the way they were and didn't ask questions. Now that I've aged, I try hard to change the things I don't like. Things are really tough right now. My heart is being torn to shreds and there is no one I can talk to about them. That is why I wrote to you Lord, you are all I have.

I want to run away but I have nowhere safe to go. Uncle Bo? Nope, doing drugs. Uncle Tom? Nope, tremendous mood swings and isn't stable. Gagga or Poppi? Nope, alcoholics. Stepdad, Jimm? Nope, drugs, and egotistical. Biological father, Barry? Nope, drugs, not stable and doesn't even know me. What about your mom, why can't you talk to her? Well, when I mention that I HATE IT when she drinks she doesn't understand. She either gets angry and takes me the wrong way or says she will "try" to stop. It never gets better and then I feel like a fool. She then just tries to hide it from me. When I question her she plays dumb and naïve.

I love my mother more than anyone on this planet but she is turning out just like everyone else in this family. I have had it with ALL the drunks and I will just die if she ends up one too. I refuse to live with another addict!

Every time she and her boyfriend fight, drinking is involved. Two immature adults making total tails of themselves who keep me up all night long. I wish there was someone I could tell who would understand. Am I being tested to see how much I can hold inside? There is about to be an eruption soon.

I had a nightmare the other night about Uncle Bo, Uncle Tom and my mom. They all died and I was left all alone. Not sure what this dream was about but all of these people have one thing in common, drugs and alcohol.

I want someone to go to church with me. Not just to make me happy but because they desire a change in their

My siblings began to act out in different ways. Alicia, ten years old, would become instantly ill when it was time to go visit Jimm. She was super clingy to my mother and needed her within sight at all times. Donnie, six years old, would have episodes where he lashed out, calling my mother horrible names. One night he asked Uncle Bo, "Do you like my Daddy?" Bo responded with a vague, "He is alright." Donnie kicked him in the shin screaming, "Well, he hates you!" My mother did her best to ignore these emotional outbursts, allowing him freedom to express himself, but eventually sought the counsel of a psychiatrist.

The psychiatrist expressed concerns that she may have "future juvenile delinquents" on her hands if actions weren't taken to curb these behaviors. He recommended she discuss these behaviors with Jimm in hopes of working together to support the children during these stressful changes. If Jimm refused to help make corrections to the children's behaviors, then visitation rights may need to be revoked or monitored. He also asked my mother a thought-provoking question. "Do the children act out more after having a visit with their father?" He sent her home with twenty-five sentence starters for Alicia and I to complete. Donnie was too young.

Here are a few:

Question	Alicia's response (10yo)	Chris's response (17yo)
Men______________	are gross	scare me
A mother__________	is the boss	is my greatest security
My greatest fear_________	is my dad	is growing up
A father____________	is not to do what mine did	is someone I want to forget

The ink was barely dry from our responses when our world turned upside down once again. Marty and my mother sat by the pool on a beautiful Saturday afternoon while my siblings swam and jumped on the trampoline with a few neighborhood children. Jimm had called earlier in the day trying to make arrangements to have the children over for the night. My mother encouraged Alicia to return his call, to which she adamantly refused.

My Mother's Journal:
I pressured Alicia a little, stating that he (Jimm) hadn't seen or talked to them in a while, and after all, he is their father. Under her breath Alicia said, "I know something you don't know." Marty overheard her and asked what it was that she knew. He quietly tried to bait it out of her but Alicia remained silent. I asked her if she'd feel better if we went inside and discussed the situation in private. We instantly locked ourselves in the bathroom and she opened up verbally.

Two of her best girl-friends told her that Jimm had played with their privates when they had spent the night. I remained calm as we talked but internally I was livid. These little girls were outside swimming in our pool. After my conversation with Alicia, I calmly spoke to each of her friends privately. Both openly expressed the same story. The touching always occurred when they were sleeping. Jimm would come in, pull their panties down and touch their genitals. If they woke up he quietly told them to go back to sleep that they were having a bad dream.

Chris called to check-in, I reluctantly shared with her what had just transpired. Her response was, "Now maybe you will believe me, Mom!"

I drove to Jimm's by myself, while Marty went to a friend's to borrow a gun for safety purposes. Grateful the fellow did not lend it. Jimm and I talked outside his trailer for approximately fifteen minutes, until Marty arrived. I was anxious to see Jimm's reaction to these new accusations.

He was uncannily calm after I shared the girl's confessions, aloofly saying they were mistaken. He was only tucking them in and tickling them to sleep, adding, "Linda, I learned that from you. The children always fall asleep so easily when you tickle their arms or back." Tension mounted when Jimm turned to Marty and abruptly said, "You better not ever abuse my children!"

The following day, another little girl who had the same experience with Jimm on a camping trip with our family came forward. My mother proceeded to talk with each of the girl's parents, notified the local police department, and asked for a professional to be sent immediately to our home.

> *My Mother's Journal:*
> *Jimm called and asked, "What have you found out? Have you had a chance to talk with the girls and their parents?" My answer was, "Yes, and you sicken me more and more by the minute." His response was, "Are you trying to scare me?" No Jimm, you need help! It sounded like he was calling from a payphone at the beach. When I questioned him, he said he was staying out of town for now.*

Despite the fact that my mother was a complete mess and consumed with guilt, she was a warrior. As HRS, the Child Protection Team, and counselors were all called in to evaluate and videotape the girl's testimonies, my mother made sure that these children would not be harassed, degraded, or humiliated. I was proud of how she handled the situation but could not help feeling angry: Angry that innocent children would be changed forever. Angry that Jimm had personally destroyed our family. Angry that these circumstances could possibly have been prevented if my personal account had been taken seriously.

he covers me

Steve Camp

Three days following the onset of this nightmare, I drove to The Sound Warehouse. The trailer Jimm had been living in, which was parked behind the building, was left unlocked and completely empty. Refrigerator doors opened and defrosted. Stereo, computer, clothing, my sibling's toys, and even his motorcycle, all gone.

I proceeded to drive to the front parking lot, pulling in beside my ex-aunt Tanya's car. When I entered the lobby, she looked shocked.

"Where is he?" My voice cracked as I desperately fought back the tears.

"I have no idea. Two hundred dollars is gone from the cash drawer, and customers are threatening to sue," she rambled. The showroom, which normally had a plethora of home stereo systems, speakers, and car stereo displays, was virtually empty. "I have had to sell things cheap just to pay the bills," she defended.

I was so confused. What was the rush? In the back of the warehouse were large mirrors that reflected the bay where car installations took place. There sat Jimm's '69 Camaro. That was all I could process and rushed out of the building weeping.

In less than one month, Tanya had sold everything. The
business had been completely gutted, and was now up for sale.

Unfortunately, after countless meetings with attorneys, there was nothing that could be done to help my mother until Jimm had been located. She was without child support or stockholder money from The Sound Warehouse. In hopes that someone would come forward with information about Jimm's whereabouts, my mother placed a missing person bulletin in the Sunday morning *News Herald*. It included a photograph of Jimm, our home phone number and the following statement "Our Dad is Missing! Please call us if you know anything."

> *My Mother's Journal:*
> *27 October, 1986*
> *The Child Protection Officer assigned to us stopped by today. She was informed that the search for Jimm continues in another case, a missing Porsche. Evidently, Jimm was working on the car Saturday the 11th when he disappeared. The plot is definitely thickening.*

An all-points bulletin and warrant for Jimm's arrest, including immediate return to Florida, was issued. There would be reports over the next few weeks that the car was spotted in California. I was numb, virtually a walking zombie. When friends asked about the newspaper post or how my family was coping, I pretended to be a worried daughter. There was no way I could tell them that the only father I had ever known and loved was involved in drugs, had molested young girls, including me, and had stolen a Porsche.

> *My Mother's Journal:*
> *9 December 1986*
> *Called the Police Dept. today to relay that Donnie had received a birthday card from Jimm postmarked Van Nuys, California.*

> *The note inside the card read:*

> *Love is forever. I love you, son. Have a Happy Birthday. Someday I'll be back. Take care of your mother and sisters. Love, Dad*

haven't got time for the pain

Carly Simon

For years, I had been negligent in following the physician's order to wear the back brace prescribed for scoliosis. It remained surreptitiously hidden in my closet when friends came over and only worn while I slept. A follow-up visit in the fall of my senior year revealed the disturbing news that the curvature had worsened to the point of needing surgical correction. The doctor explained, if left untreated, there would be problems in adulthood with childbearing and pain management. Unfortunately, there was no money or health insurance to cover these expenses.

My mother was referred to Dr. Flynn, a pediatric orthopedic surgeon in Orlando, Florida. He was a specialist in pediatric spinal surgeries, and performed numerous surgeries a month for the Florida Elks Children's Hospital. This charitable organization supported children with musculoskeletal conditions, postoperative burns, and spinal cord injuries. To be eligible for admission, the patient must be a resident of the state of Florida, between the ages of birth to seventeen years old, and have an orthopedic condition or problem. The Elks would pick up all costs for the surgery and post-operative care if approved. There was an urgency in getting all the paperwork in since I was turning eighteen in two months.

To our surprise, we were notified within two weeks that surgery had been scheduled in Orlando, Florida, on February 10th. Correcting the curvature would include a spinal fusion from T-10 to L-3. The surgeon would permanently connect these vertebrae by shaving bone from my hip and placing it between the bones. This technique mimics the healing process of broken bones; however, two Cotrel-Dubousset rods along with plates and screws would be secured above and below this fusion in order for that section of the spine to heal as one solid unit.

There were a few risks that caused anxiety and many sleepless nights. The first was the need for numerous blood transfusions due to the loss of blood during the surgery. Fortunately, prior to leaving for Orlando, I was able to donate two pints of my own blood. This also mitigated complications like infection and rejection. The second risk was permanent nerve damage which could cause loss of strength or sensation to my legs. Although the percentages were extremely low for paralysis, the fact that it was even a possibility instilled tremendous fear.

Tension mounted as the countdown to my surgery date rapidly approached. We were told to plan for a two-week stay in

Orlando. My mother scrambled to make arrangements for my siblings, our pets, house plants, and mail.

Unfortunately, her boyfriend, Marty, felt ignored. He had become accustomed to her attention and now was drinking alone. The toxic mix of alcohol consumption and his jealous nature fueled an explosive argument a few days before our departure. I was jolted from a deep sleep to Marty screaming horrible things at my mother. I marched downstairs and boldly yelled in his face, "Get Out!" He was so intoxicated he could hardly walk. Fight or flight had kicked in and for the first time in my life it was "fight" that propelled me to begin pushing this grown man out of our door. As I made one last shove through the doorway, he spun around with venom on his tongue and said, "I hope you're paralyzed!"

> *My Mother's Journal:*
> *Don't care to see or hear from Marty ever again. He has hurt this family mentally and physically beyond recognition. It is definitely going to take time, understanding, and a lot of love to repair the damage he has created. I can no longer deal with his problems and my own.*
>
> *"Hope you're paralyzed!" the words spoken to Chris without thought under the influence and then denting her truck with a forceful kick. These words and actions will not be easily forgotten.*
>
> *Why is Chris such a threat to the men in my life? Is it because they are jealous of our close relationship? Do I show her more attention than them? Or is it because they are younger men and they can't stand a seventeen year old who is more mature than they are?*

As much as his words stung deeply, I was thanking Jesus for answered prayers. He had made a way for me to have a critical surgery that my mother could not afford, simultaneously eliminating another man from my mother's life that was poisoning our family. I was clinging to what Jesus said in Luke 18:27, "What is impossible for people is possible with Jesus."(NLT) I had to trust that my health was in His hands too.

Even though I was fifteen pounds lighter, the surgery was a success and we were home in two weeks. At eighteen years old, I weighed a measly eighty-five pounds. Although there was a significant amount of pain and stiffness, it was the itching from an allergic reaction to the tape, that caused the most grief. Restrictions for the next few months included no lifting, twisting, bending, or driving. For seven weeks, my teachers came to the house or sent assignments home with friends. When I returned for the last month of school, the textbooks were too heavy and the hard desk chairs caused bursitis on my spine. To alleviate these issues and keep me in school, I cruised around campus in a wheelchair for the remainder of the year.

> *My Mother's Journal:*
> *31 May 1987*
> *Well, although it is a beautiful morning, it has not begun favorably for me. It is Senior Recognition Day at the First Baptist Church. I was up at 4:30 am fearing I would oversleep and miss the prayer breakfast to honor the graduates. My shower went smoothly, the make-up flowed on easily and my hair even fell into place without much difficulty; however, I now find myself stuffed in a slip like the skin on a sausage. I am literally trapped in a dress which may have to be surgically removed from my body. The sleeves are embedded so deeply into my arms that the blood flow has been stifled and a bluish hue can be seen from my elbow to fingertips. I am color coordinated as my arms now match the blue stripes on my dress. I don't know how much longer I can exist in this tightly bound environment. I feel numbness setting in, Chris better hurry up!*

The timing of my surgery was obviously precious protection from God. It kept me from the temptations my peers were facing during Spring Break and graduation parties. My spine needed healing which forced me to rest physically, emotionally, and spiritually. Just getting dressed and being upright for a few hours wiped me out. Therefore, much of my time was spent in my room reading the Bible, journaling, praying, and setting goals for my future. This sounds super cheesy, but I also began writing prayers and letters to my unknown husband. If I were to ever marry, I wanted Jesus to be the anchor.

For a graduation gift, my mother bought me a roundtrip plane ticket to California to visit childhood friends. Arrangements were made for me to stay with my mother's best friend, Edwina Patterson, and her family. She and her husband Floyd had five children. When we lived in California, our families loved to hang out at the park for Saturday picnics or backyard barbecues. Our parents would sit for hours watching us perform skits and musicals on the swing set in the backyard.

Prior to leaving on my trip, I began asking questions again about my biological father, Barry Ray. I knew that in previous years, he had lived in California. Maybe, if he was still living there, this would be a good time to meet him.

Christon - Drum Major

Christon's Senior Prom

in the air tonight

Phil Collins

The future looked bright as I soared 30,000 feet in an airplane headed to Los Angeles, California. With a troublesome year behind me, a summer away from home would be good for my soul. The first week in sunny California was uneventful. We relaxed at the beach, shopped, and drove past my old elementary school and home. Towards the end of the second week, my mother called informing me she had located Barry's address in Hollywood, California.

There was a lot of fear and trepidation about meeting Barry, who I referred to as my biological sperm donor. My mother left him when I was nine months old and I had not seen or spoken to him, or members of his family, since. I knew nothing about his childhood, siblings, or parents. The only connection I had to this man was a few photographs of us together in a park when I was an infant. On top of that, I knew nothing about his current condition or lifestyle. Would he be strung out on drugs, say inappropriate things, or verbally bash my mother? I longed to meet him but did not want a confrontation. Edwina listened to my angst, assuring me that I would be safe with her in control. There was no doubt in my mind that this five-foot-two Burmese firecracker could handle Barry Ray.

My mother had met Edwina a few years after marrying Jimm, they were co-workers at a local bank. Although she did not know

Barry, she understood the longing to have a relationship with your father. At twelve years old, living in Burma, her father died of a brain tumor, leaving her mother to raise five children alone. Not long after her father's death, Edwina's mother packed a few suitcases and bravely boarded an airplane to the United States with her children to start a new life. When I questioned whether it was wise to meet Barry, she encouraged me to take the risk, not wanting me to live with regrets.

Arrangements were made for the two of us to drive to Hollywood unannounced. This would be staged as a friendly drop-in. Edwina would tell Barry that Linda, my mother, had asked her to check-in on him if she were ever in the area. I would pose as her daughter with no intention of exposing my true identity. This plan would give me an opportunity to see Barry organically. No pressure on either one of us.

Barry lived on Hollywood Boulevard. Two miles west of his apartment were famous landmarks like the Hollywood Wax Museum, Madame Tussauds, the Hollywood Walk of Fame, and the iconic Chinese Theater. As we parked the car, it was very clear that we needed to be out of this area before the sun went down. This was skid row, something I had only seen in movies.

His small apartment building was wedged in between two businesses. As we entered, we saw a staircase situated at the back wall of the lobby. I was flooded with a sense of foreboding as we climbed the stairs. The eerie stillness and musty mildew smell continued down a long carpeted hallway lined with doors on either side. We stopped in front of the door labeled 206. This was it. My heart was beating so fast I thought it might explode as Edwina knocked. Second guessing whether this was a good idea, I silently prayed, "God, maybe it would be best if he isn't home. Especially if this is dangerous or if it will cause me more pain. Please help me breathe, I feel like I'm going to pass out."

The door slowly opened, and there stood Barry Ray, my biological father. As planned, Edwina told Barry that she was Linda's best friend. She and her daughter (me) were in the area and wanted to check in on him. He kindly invited us into his apartment where Edwina and Barry stood chatting for approximately fifteen minutes.

I was so consumed with keeping myself vertical and breathing that their conversation sounded like the voices of the adults in a Charlie Brown cartoon, "wah wa wa wah." Instead, I focused on superficial things like my surroundings and Barry's appearance.

The one bedroom apartment was tidy with a hippie vibe. There were no photographs of friends or family but a Marilyn Monroe poster hung on a nearby wall. To my surprise, he did not appear high or even look like a drug addict. His clothes were clean and modest: a loose button up shirt, tight jeans, and black boots up to his calves. *What is that tattoo I see vaguely on his right forearm? I would never learn what that tattoo was however, years later I was informed he had a tattoo of a sailboat on his right shoulder.* Numerous silver rings donned his fingers, along with a silver chain that hung loosely around his neck.

Did I resemble him? Maybe his slender frame or his small pug nose that held up circular John Lennon glasses. I was snapped out of my investigations when I heard goodbyes being exchanged. "I'm sorry, what was your name?" Barry repeated to me, extending his hand.

No way, could this really be happening? "My name is Christon Ray," I blurted without thought. Immediately, uncontrollable tears began streaming down my face.

Gasping he said, "I knew it the moment I saw you. Can I hug you?" As we embraced for the first time, there were no words.

I was a complete mess the entire ride back to the Patterson's home. Mentally berating myself for showing emotion in front of him. I did not want Barry to think that my life had been incomplete without his presence. I had survived just fine.

I still had another month in California, but after meeting Barry, I felt an urgency to return home. Post traumatic stress had kicked in, landing me in bed for three days with body aches and high fevers. There were so many people in and out of the Patterson home that I couldn't process my thoughts and emotions. My anxiety escalated daily and sleeping became difficult. I would awake in a cold sweat, crying uncontrollably from nightmares. I would see a glimpse of Jimm and then poof he would be gone. These nightmares produced an undercurrent of anxiety that Jimm was waiting for the right opportunity to jump out of the shadows and hurt me. Although these nightmares were unfounded, it was my mind's way of processing the meeting with Barry mixed with the uncertain whereabouts of Jimm. Emotionally drained and physically exhausted, my flight was bumped up a few weeks. This girl needed her mommy!

Once home, I was able to think more clearly and ask myself some hard questions: *What defines me? Is it the approval or love of a father?* Hopefully not, because both Barry and Jimm were a complete disappointment in paternal security. *Who am I? Is my identity found in my name?* If so, I am a lost cause because both my first and last names have changed multiple times over the last eighteen years. I was born Christon Ray but my mother called me Christy. As I entered middle school, I thought Christy sounded childish, so I asked people to call me Chris. Jimm had illegally changed my last name in kindergarten, which remained throughout high school. It was even printed on my high school diploma. What would my name be as I entered this new chapter of my life? Returning to my legal birth name, Christon Ray, made the most sense as I applied for college scholarships and financial aid. This was on all legal documents like my birth certificate, social security card, and driver's license. It was important that my life from this point forward be firmly founded *on Christ*, so returning to *Christon* gave me a connection to the Lord. Praise God that not even my name was a mistake.

As I wrestled with these questions, it all began to make sense when I read Psalm 139:13-18 (NLT) "You (God) made all the delicate, inner parts of my body and knit me together in my mother's womb. Thank you for making me so wonderfully complex! Your workmanship is marvelous- how well I know it. You watched me as I was being formed in utter seclusion, as I was woven together in the dark of the womb. You saw me before I was born. Every day of my life was recorded in your book. Every moment was laid out before a single day had passed. How precious are your thoughts about me, O God. They cannot be numbered! I can't even count them; they outnumber the grains of sand!"

I was in awe of the fact that the God of the universe had taken the time to create every minuscule detail of my body, from each freckle placement, which I have thousands, to my five million hair follicles. He didn't create me and toss me to the side. He made me so that we could have an intimate relationship. Every single day, He is thinking precious thoughts about me and recording my activities in a scrapbook. I am no longer alone. For the first time in my life, I no longer searched for love, security, or a surname in an earthly father, I had all that I needed in my Heavenly Father. I was a child of God.

pray for me

Michael W. Smith

The summer before I started classes at the local community college my youth pastor, Poker, asked if I would be interested in working a few church camps. College students would be responsible for leading small groups, organizing fun games and activities, and most importantly, building relationships with the high school students who came to the camp. I had never attended a church camp in high school, but knew this opportunity could be life changing. The Bible teaching, worship, and people were a breath of fresh air. I loved listening to the student's stories and encouraging them that a relationship with Jesus changes everything.

While I was working at the church youth camps, my mother made the agonizing decision to sell our family home. Struggling to provide as a single parent, our home had become a tremendous financial burden. Although downsizing into an apartment meant sharing a room with my little sister, it did have many positives. We were now just a few miles from the beach, mall, community college, and my mother's workplace.

Strolling in from an afternoon college lab, I was shocked to see Marty, my mother's old flame, relaxing on our couch. Marty instantly saw the anger on my face, humbly asking if I would sit and hear him out. Over the previous nine months he had been incarcerated for another DUI. Sober and sorry, he was asking for another chance. He genuinely loved my mother and having a man in the house could provide some stability. I hated myself for doubting that he was capable of following through on his promises. *How could I deny extending forgiveness to this man when I myself had been forgiven repeatedly?* This was a perfect opportunity for me to show my family how much God loved them. When Marty finished talking, I shared numerous concerns I had about their relationship. The only way I saw a future with them as a couple was if they put God first and eliminated alcohol. Primarily, for my mother's sake, I talked about their security and identity not being in each other but in the Lord. They listened intently, verbalizing their desire to have a healthy relationship with God and each other. There were lots of tears as we hugged, forgave each other, and prayed together. It was a beautiful moment, leaving me hopeful that this would be a life-changing milestone for our family.

It was wishful thinking to assume their sobriety would last. Their dysfunctional cycle resumed a few months later. Protecting my siblings, a full load of college classes, working weekends at the local emergency room, and many nights having to babysit two drunk adults, was weighing heavily on me. I finally pushed aside the guilt of betraying my mother and sought counsel from Poker. "It is not your responsibility to take care of your siblings, Christon. You are not their mother. The best thing you could do for your mother and for yourself is to go away to college. It will force her to take responsibility for her life and her children."

I knew Poker was right, but putting this into action seemed impossible. *How would I pay for college? Who would take care of my siblings when things went sideways?* The guilt of leaving them surrounded by dysfunctional adults was overwhelming. I began praying that if this was the direction God wanted me to take that He would open doors and fill me with peace.

For Spring Break, I went to Virginia to visit my childhood friend, Theresa Hawkins. While there, I received a tearful phone call from my mother explaining that she and Marty had broken up for good. The pain in her voice was palpable as she relayed the sequence of events. "Things got really out of hand tonight, Twink. We were having a great time barbequing and drinking by the pool when Marty began demanding that I cover up my swimsuit. When I asked why, he became extremely aggressive in front of everyone. Uncle Bo tried to calm him down but this only escalated Marty's anger. I thought he was going inside to gather his things; however, he returned with an arrow in his hunting bow and pointed it directly at Bo."

Jealous outbursts were common for Marty when alcohol was involved but this time was different. He was hell-bent on killing someone. In an effort to protect her brother, she jumped in front of the weapon attempting to break the arrow. Sadly, the arrow released from the bow and stabbed my mother in the arm. In a panic, Marty took off in my Ford Ranger while my mother was rushed to the hospital. Relieved that there was no muscle or bone damage, she was sutured up and sent home. Later that evening, she was informed that Marty had been arrested for another DUI after crashing my truck into a telephone pole.

I was thankful that despite a totaled vehicle, the evening did not end tragically however, my frustration with my mother was at an all-time high. Would she ever break the unhealthy cycle? Her poor choices were creating unnecessary fear and anxiety in her children. She was all we had. My mother was embarrassed, heartbroken, and disgusted with herself for falling victim to a man once again but instead of dealing with her guilt and pain in healthy ways, she continued to numb out nightly with alcohol. It was obvious to me that things had to change. I could not continue to put the pieces of her life back together and still try to begin my own.

A dream of mine since childhood was to become a pediatrician. Yet, after exploring the years it would take to become a physician and the outrageous cost of medical school, I decided pediatric nursing would be a better option for me. I applied to a few colleges out of state with nursing programs, praying that if this was God's plan, He would make a way. I clung to Proverbs 3:5-6 (NLT) which says, "Trust in the Lord with all your heart; do not depend on your own understanding. Seek His will in all you do, and he will show you which path to take."

To my surprise, I was accepted into the Ida V. Moffett School of Nursing at Samford University in Birmingham, Alabama.

Although there were still many unanswered details like roommates, transportation, and finances, I was eager to begin this new chapter of my life. I had a deep inner peace, despite many family members scoffing over the school's tuition.

> *Excerpt from letter:*
> *To: My Future Husband*
> *From: Christon*
> *August 1988*
> *I have so much going on right now that my brain feels boggled. I leave in three days for college. I am so nervous and scared. The Lord just keeps beating FAITH, FAITH, FAITH into my head. I know I have the faith that He will work things out, I just need to rest in it.*

I was so excited when Theresa Hawkins decided to transfer to Samford. Naturally we became roommates. Neither of us had visited the campus prior to our move-in date, only seeing a few pictures from our acceptance packet. We were both blown away by Samford's beauty.

Since I no longer had a vehicle and my mother was unable to get off of work, transportation was my next hurdle. Fortunately, a girl who worked summer camps with me attended Birmingham Southern. The date she was heading back aligned perfectly with the date I needed to be on campus. Never thinking to ask the size of her car or if others would be traveling with us, I was stunned when she pulled up in a VW Bug with two other girls. Trying not to panic, I quickly unloaded my suitcases and shoved everything I was taking to college into two large trash bags. The crazy looks I received from parents and students when I walked into the dorm carrying trash bags while they carried beautiful trunks, furniture, microwaves and fun dorm decor.

Financial aid would be a faith builder for months. Knowing I would receive a Pell Grant and a few other small scholarships my first semester, there were still thousands of dollars yet to be covered. Once I had settled on campus, my free time was spent in the Financial Aid Office, scouring through huge scholarship books. If I met any of the qualifications, I would send a letter or fill out the application. In the meantime, I was attending classes while praying, "Lord, please make a way for me to stay. I love it here and want my family to see that you do the impossible."

> *Excerpt from letter:*
> *To: My Future Husband*
> *From: Christon*
> *January 1989*
> *I need God to show up. If I don't come up with three thousand dollars by Friday, Samford is going to drop my Spring classes. God has eased my worries and helped me to take things one step at a time. I have peace that He will take care of me.*

A few days later, I was notified by Financial Aid that my account was paid in full for the semester. On top of that, they informed me that I would be receiving the same scholarships and grants for the following school year. I was humbled by God's goodness to me. He had done "immeasurably more than I could have ever imagined." (Ephesians 3:20 NIV) *Thank you God for showing up!*

Long distance phone calls were expensive, so I rarely received them from home to just chat. When my mother did call, she often reported on any updated news of Jimm's whereabouts, poor decisions family members had made, or disciplinary problems with my siblings. On occasion, my thirteen-year-old sister did sneak a few calls to me. Tearfully she expressed concerns over our mother's increasing drinking habits. I loved hearing their voices, but these phone calls left me feeling anxious and helpless. Satan was doing all he could to wage war on my mind. I became consumed with worry, guilt, and fear which was a huge distraction from my studies and walk with Jesus. Every time the phone rang in my dorm room, I silently prayed for God to give me strength.

One evening after my mother had a few drinks, she called Barry Ray, my biological father. At some point in the conversation, she decided to share my school address and phone number with him. Big mistake! This lead to numerous letters that were illegible, not to mention random collect phone calls at all hours of the night. I specifically remember one call when he said he was sitting in a satellite dish, insanely rambling from one thought to the next. I called my mother the following morning, furious that she had given my personal information to a man who clearly had mental problems.

> *Excerpt from letter:*
> *To: Barry*
> *From: Linda*
> *Spring 1989*
> *It is against my better judgment to write to you but, I must express the way I feel in a manner as honest and sincere as humanly possible. I supported and even encouraged Christon's hunt for you and was delighted for her when your whereabouts were finally discovered. I'm not feeling all that positive currently, sorry to say! We have asked nothing from you in 19 years, emotionally or financially. Yet, this is what she has received from you so far:*
> *1. Letters which take a psychiatrist to decipher*
> *2. A box of meaningless junk*
> *3. Collect calls. If you wish to talk with Chris, you pay! Get your "poop" together! You are a man, with so much talent it is sickening! Stop blaming other people for your own failures. You were surrounded by love, but rejected it all. Chris could use a father who cares.*

My first year at Samford was wrapping up and I felt stronger than I ever had, but feared returning home for the summer might set me back. After much prayer, I decided to join a ministry called Campus Outreach for a summer mission project. This opportunity would allow me to be surrounded by other college students all seeking to grow deeper in their relationship with God and learn how to share my faith. My team was assigned to Panama City Beach. *Isn't it just like God to send me to the same area that had caused me tremendous pain and rejection?*

During our personal time, I would tote my bible, notebook, and Walkman radio down to the ocean and journal for hours. Why did my heart feel so heavy and dirty? Jeremiah 33:3 says, "Call to me and I will answer you and tell you great and unsearchable things you do not know." (NIV) I had no idea how deep the roots of anger and unforgiveness had grown. The secret grudges I held against so many were choking out the joy and peace God desired for me. It became crystal clear that God wanted me to forgive them, specifically Jimm. This felt impossible, yet I knew He wasn't asking me to do something He had not already done. I committed to pray for Jimm every day that summer. It sounds so easy, but in the beginning it was agony. My short dull prayers were an act of obedience only. But by the end of the summer, I was weeping over his lost soul.

When the mission project ended, I went home to regroup for a few weeks before heading back to Samford. One afternoon, my sister ran into the apartment crying as she flung mail all over the kitchen counters. Three years of silence were broken. Jimm had written each of us a letter. Little did I know, God had been preparing me for this moment all summer.

> *To: Chris*
> *From: Jimm*
> *August 1989*
> *Dear Chris,*
> *For the past three years, I've tried to forget the past. I thought I had started my life all over again, but my past is with me every day, and you are part of it. I thought it would be easy to forget everyone, and everything, but I can't. I think back often to the days when we were a family, and my life and time was devoted to you, your mom, Alicia, and Donnie. I was never happier.*
>
> *I'm not quite sure when it all started falling apart, but I know now, there are many things I wouldn't do again. Believe it or not, I was still growing up. The responsibilities I was carrying got the best of me. I realize it's my own fault, and I'm not making excuses, just letting you know how I feel.*
>
> *Just before I left Panama City, I think you and I were beginning to develop a good relationship. Not a child-parent but more of an adult-adult thing. I'm sure you have matured into a great young woman, with a life I'd be proud of.*
>
> *Since I left, I have placed myself in isolation from family, friends, and materialism. Giving me time to think and put my life back together. Time is moving quite slow for me. It's taken three years to get in touch with my inner feelings. Something I lost in Panama City.*

Due to my circumstances, I've been living an obscure "underground" type of lifestyle. My jobs are menial, I live cheap and have no motorized transportation. But I am getting by. I am in the process of facing up to my actions and trying to clear up my legal problems.

Hang in there Chris, I'm sure things aren't easy for you either, but time has a way of smoothing out the rough spots. I really miss you. There is a certain spark of life very unique to you that I have loved since our lives first came together when you were four years old. I may not have conceived you, but for most of your life and the better part of mine, I helped you learn, taught you right from wrong, and watched you grow and mature.

I pray you haven't forgotten the good times, or hate me for the bad ones. I so want to be a part of your life again, so you can have a Daddy and I can have my "big girl" back. I can't help out financially now, but that time is coming. I hope one day you will be able to depend on me again. I'll never stop loving you. You will always be my daughter, no matter what happens to my life or yours. If you want to write to me, send letters to my sister. She will hold them for me. I haven't told anyone where I live and I must keep it that way until I sort out my problems with the law.
Take care Chris, True love lasts forever, Daddy

Excerpt from letter:
To: Jimm
From: Linda
The children were all astounded to hear from you; although I knew that one day you would make an attempt to communicate with them. You have three wonderfully different youngsters. All three reacted in their own separate ways to the letters received. For example: Alicia, who was the one to check the mailbox and the first to read ALL the letters, became hysterical. She possesses a tremendous amount of hostility towards you. So thankful that Chris was home from college to console and comfort her little sister. The "Twink" reacted in her typical angelic manner, saying, "Maybe

---

The rest of the eight page letter I wrote to Jimm detailed
important milestones he had missed in my life: my back surgery,
prom, graduation, college, but most importantly, my relationship with
Jesus.

when i'm back on my feet again

Michael Bolton

The next few years, my focus was on hospital clinicals, passing my classes, and the upcoming NCLEX-RN. There was very little time for a social life and dating was nonexistent. The stress was overwhelming at times. Many exams covered over twenty chapters, making my head feel like it was going to explode. One of the most difficult classes required for my degree was microbiology. The professor was physically and intellectually intimidating. She towered over the students in a starched white lab coat, her facial features in a permanent botox scowl and hair tightly bound in a bun. Our class would be deeply entrenched in our lab experiments when she would loudly proclaim her disgust, the smell of a particular organism like "staphylococcus aureus" burning. We would scramble to make sure we were not the responsible party.

Nursing students at Samford had the option of taking the NCLEX-RN (State Licensure Exam) halfway through the program or waiting until their bachelor's degree was complete. I chose to take the test early in hopes of being able to work as an RN as I finished my degree. With the help of a notable review course and lots of prayers, I passed.

Excerpt from letter:
To: My Future Husband
From: Christon
May 1991
*Well, one of the biggest things of my life happened, I
became a Registered Nurse. I can't even describe to you the
excitement I feel. I screamed and yelled for a whole day.
Now that the excitement has worn off the reality is beginning
to sink in. I begin my first job as an RN in one week. I am
scared, insecure, anxious, and worried. I know that most
of these negatives are a fear of the unknown. Working
with pediatric oncology patients will be very sad, but I am
praying that God will give me the strength to be a backbone
for these children and give them hope.*

Up to this point, I had relied on classmates or friends for
transportation; this included church, clinicals, fast food runs, and
even when I wanted to go home. My part-time income as an RN
allowed me the opportunity to purchase a used Honda Civic. Having
my own car gave me more freedom and flexibility, especially when
it came to school breaks. I often stayed in Birmingham to work or
traveled to be a youth intern with Poker at his new church in Oviedo,
Florida.

Excerpt from letter:
To: Christon
From: Mom
Dear Twink,
*Really can't stand the thought of you being out of school
and spending your summer with another family, especially
when we need and love you so. Don't get me wrong, I'm
proud of you and know you made a commitment to Poker. It
would have been nice to have you here one summer. Guess
I'm slightly jealous of having to always share "my angel." I
realize you have so much to offer, especially when all that is
here is imperfection. I just miss you!*

As I entered my senior year at Samford, I couldn't wait to
graduate and begin my life as an adult. I was confident that I would

stay in Birmingham, work full-time at the hospital, and get an apartment. For the first time, I felt like I was in control of my future. "If you think you are standing strong, be careful not to fall. The temptations in your life are no different from what others experience. And God is faithful. He will not allow the temptation to be more than you can stand. When you are tempted, he will show you a way out so that you can endure." (1 Corinthians 10:12-13 NLT)

When I returned home for Christmas break it was immediately apparent that my grandmother, Gagga, was not doing well. My mother blamed her illness on stress and had seen the storm brewing for some time. The constant whirlwind of bailing her family members out of messes and keeping it a secret had taken its toll on her mind and body.

> *My Mother's Journal:*
> *October 1991*
> *Mom (Gagga) is not doing well, she is short and curt on the phone every evening with me. In some ways she has brought this on herself by never being able to say no. She is always there, always available, protecting and secluding her family, never allowing anyone, even her husband (Poppi), to know there are problems within. She continues to cover up his actions (alcohol use) as well. It is time for her to realize that she cannot do it alone and that others have skeletons in their closets too. I know of no one who is perfect.*

A few weeks before Christmas, my grandmother was admitted to the hospital in a delusional state. Her body was trembling with uncontrollable spasms as her wide eyes darted wildly from one sight, sound, or movement in the room to another. Minutes later she would relax, tossing her head from side to side as if to rid herself of an undesirable thought. She fidgeted with the top of her sheet, folding it back and forth like children do when making a fan. The next few days were filled with a battery of tests and procedures. All of her results were normal, leaving the specialists baffled. Sadly, my sweet Gagga continued to tensely jerk and speak incoherently. Verbalization was difficult, and she was unable to complete sentences or thoughts. She was disturbed by visits from floating pencils, clocks without faces, buttermilk in her bed, and an eight foot man, to mention only a few of her hallucinations.

> *My Mother's Journal:*
> *December 1991*
> *Seeing her helpless, frightened frame having to be positioned in bed was so difficult. There has been a slight improvement even though the hallucinations continue. She is becoming aware of the fact that she is having difficulty. For example, after reaching out to grab an imaginary object, she'd say "see, it's not even there" or after one visitor left the room she said, "He was by himself, wasn't he?" I responded, "Yes, Mom, why?" She replied, "Well, I saw five people, three were black and two were white." Her hallucinations are so detailed, so real, that it is making it difficult for her to sleep. She cried when they gave her a sleeping pill this evening, fearing her vivid dreams or that she would be lost forever in an imaginary world of "La La land," never to wake up.*

We were hopeful of the progress she was making. Over the next few days, all her meals were consumed, coordination was improving, and she was able to shuffle down the hall with little assistance. In my twenty-two years, I had never seen my grandmother without her gorgeous auburn hair brushed, braided, and tied up in a bun. She always had on fresh make-up, a trendy outfit, and absolutely never left the house without lipstick. When she began asking for her brush and lipstick we all thought a discharge from the hospital was imminent.

When I arrived at the hospital Christmas morning, it was encouraging to see Gagga sitting up in bed, hair braided and make-up donned. As we chatted she shared her disappointment in failing to finish the Christmas shopping. With perfect clarity she communicated what gifts I was to purchase and wrap for each family member. I hugged and kissed her as I left, promising to accomplish everything on her list. Together we would make this Christmas special despite the delay in our celebration.

Unfortunately, my grandmother suffered a massive stroke in the middle of the night, passing away the following afternoon. The autopsy revealed that both carotid arteries were severely blocked. The loss was overwhelming.

> *Excerpt from letter:*
> *To: Uncle Bob and Aunt Betty*
> *From: Linda*
> *I know people say "life goes on," but we (Dad, Chris, and myself) are having an extremely difficult time adjusting to life without Mom. As you know, Dad and Mom were inseparable. Needless to say, Dad is a very lonely man. He visits her gravesite daily, reaches out to hold her hand, and calls her name from time to time. Naturally, the most empty of times for him are the night hours when they would snuggle and cuddle. In Chris' case, Gagga and she had so much in common. They had the same body frame, shoe size, and style. A few months ago, Chris wore one of Mom's dresses she had made in Japan, it fit her perfectly. They had the same personality right down to their positives and negatives about men. As for me, my mother was my best friend!*

My grandfather, Poppi, was completely lost. He had not written a check in forty-nine years nor did he know what bills they had to pay. My grandmother did all the cooking so even working the microwave was a new task. Truthfully, the only thing he was confident in performing without her was using the television remote control and driving. In order to help with this transition, I moved in with Poppi until my classes resumed in February.

Returning to finish my last semester at Samford was bittersweet. Although I needed to get back to work at the hospital and buckle down in my final nursing classes, my brain felt cloudy. I still grieved the loss of my grandmother and couldn't shake the guilt of leaving my grandfather alone. On top of that, I was distracted with thoughts of Randy.

Randy and I had been friends since eighth grade. There was never anything romantic between us. As a matter of fact, I dated a few of his close friends in high school. Randy's father passed away in November, a month before my grandmother. So while I was home we reconnected, sharing our grief and pain on long drives or walks on the beach. He had a reputation for being the fun-lovin', crazy, outgoing party boy, always ready to take a risk or plunge into a new adventure. However, the death of his father had sent him into a tailspin, forcing him to ask deep questions about life, his future, and God. I felt comfortable confiding my pain and grief to Randy because he had known my dysfunctional family for years.

> *Excerpt from letter:*
> *To: My Future Husband*
> *From: Christon*
> *You have been in my prayers a lot lately. Most of my best friends are in exclusive relationships, two are recently engaged. Honestly, I don't want to be single. God, please help me with contentment, I want to wait for your best.*

One evening in March, exhausted from working a twelve-hour shift at the hospital, I came home to a startling message left on my answering machine. It was an unfamiliar male voice stating that he was an officer from the Los Angeles County Police Department. He left his direct line on the recording and asked that I call as soon as possible in reference to Barry Ray. My heart sank, as all sorts of questions flooded my brain: Had Barry been arrested and if so for what? Did he overdose on drugs? How did the L.A.P.D. get my phone number? My whole body was shaking as I attempted to dial the number.

> *Los Angeles Police Department*
> *Death Investigation Report*
> *25 March 1992*
> *The victim was identified by his distinctive tattoos as Barry Ray the missing tenant from apartment #206. The victim was found stabbed to death and stuffed in a cardboard box, adjacent to the trash dumpsters, in the driveway of his apartment building.*

This bombshell enveloped me in an avalanche of unexpected emotions: shock, disbelief, sadness, anger, regret, guilt, disgust. It was an emptiness I had never experienced. I was so angry with myself for weeping and not being able to pull myself together. Barry Ray, after all, was just my sperm donor. He had never put a bandaid on one of my "boo boo's," cheered me on at a ballgame, or bought me a sweet treat after a long day at school. Why was I so messed up over someone who I had only met once? Although it hurt me to think of the gruesome way his life was taken, the truth of my pain was in the loss of hope. No matter how absent or dysfunctional a father may be, every little girl holds on to hope that one day he will show up, clean up, or fess up. I grieved the father figure that would never be. I no longer had a choice to have hope, it was taken from me.

In the midst of my second loss in three months, it was Randy who showed up. Not only did he drive to campus to check on me, but he was calling almost nightly, sending flowers, and writing letters frequently. It was apparent that he wanted to be more than friends, and truthfully his attention was a comforting distraction. Not long after we were officially dating, Randy enlisted in the Navy in hopes of becoming a Navy Seal. For months we dated long distance. He graduated from basic training around the same time that I graduated from Samford with my Bachelors of Science in Nursing.

Shortly after moving into my first apartment in Birmingham, I flew to California to visit Randy before he began Basic Underwater Demolition Seal (BUDS) Training. We rode horses bareback on the beaches of Tijuana, strolled through quaint shops on Coronado Island, and enjoyed a gorgeous sunset on a dinner cruise. At the end of the cruise, Randy got down on one knee, opened a small box revealing a diamond ring, and asked if I would marry him. Completely taken off guard, I responded, "Yes," ignoring the uncertainty I felt on the inside.

Within a month I had decided that I would move to California to be closer to Randy as he finished up Seal Training. My Honda Civic was packed to the brim as Theresa and I pulled onto the interstate heading West. We were on a tight schedule, my first day of orientation at San Diego Children's Hospital was in five days. Thankfully, Theresa was our navigator and we were not dependent on my incompetent navigational skills. Safely arriving in just three days to the studio apartment I had rented, we booked Theresa's return flight to Birmingham. Reality began to sink in as I watched my best friend disappear into the crowded airport. I was alone.

The past seven months had been a roller coaster and I was bankrupt emotionally and spiritually. I had been stiff-arming the Lord, forging my own path, making major life-changes without even consulting Him. Something had to change, I couldn't stand the chasm I felt between Lord and I. Contemporary Christian music artist Susan Ashton wrote a song titled "Grand Canyon" which perfectly illustrated the current condition of my heart.

My first day of orientation was uneventful, but the traffic to and from the hospital was insane. I returned to the apartment to clean up, anxious about seeing Randy for the first time since I had arrived. When he walked through the door, it was clear to me that this was not my future husband. The conversation to follow was incredibly painful as I returned the ring and we said goodbye.

There was no way that I was staying in California now that our relationship was over. Immediately after receiving wired money from my mother, I packed my car once again and began the two thousand mile trek home to Panama City. There were no cell phones or GPS devices. It was me, a map, and God. Although admittedly fearful about doing this journey solo, it proved to be just what my broken heart needed: uninterrupted time to cry out to my Savior asking Him to forgive me for drifting so far away.

There was never any contact with Randy again until I received this unexpected email twenty years later:

To: Christon
From: Randy
2011
I reached out to your sister on Facebook and she gave me
your email. There is a reason why I am contacting you now.
As selfish as it may seem, I have thought of you every day for
twenty years, wondering where you were and how you were
doing. I loved you and our friendship. I have hated myself
for how I treated you. You always supported me but I quit on
you, the Seals and eventually many other things in my life. I
remember you talking about your father and I did everything
you hated about him. I am so sorry. Please forgive me.

Christon - Nursing School

Barry Ray

Christon wearing
Gagga's Dresses

look me in the eye

Margaret Becker

God's plan for my future was a mystery and it was obvious that I was unqualified to manage it alone. Humbled by what I saw as a colossal failure only magnified my dependence on my Heavenly Father. From that point on, I did not want to take a single step forward without asking God first.

To my mother's chagrin, when I returned home from California, I immediately began applying to children's hospitals in the southeast, praying for discernment on where to land. If she had her way, I would live at home, work locally, and help her parent my teenage siblings. Despite the guilt trip, the years away had given me enough clarity to get out of Panama City as quickly as possible.

With my prayers answered and the car packed for the third time in four months, I was off to Orlando, Florida. Arnold Palmer Children's Hospital had hired me for the night shift in their Critical Care Step Down Unit. The diversity in ages and diagnosis of the patients challenged me in new ways. On my first day, an eight-pound, two-year-old boy who we called Green Bean, stole my heart. He was given this nickname because when you held him he was as tiny as a green bean. Born premature, his lungs never fully developed, resulting in a plethora of medical issues. He had been on a ventilator since birth, making him a long-term resident of our Unit. Green Bean was my buddy, and I would beg the charge nurse to assign him to my care every time I worked.

I plugged into the church where I had attended two years earlier when I had been a summer intern with Poker. For the first few months in Orlando, a family from my Sunday School class graciously let me stay in their guest room. It didn't take long before I had saved enough money and was settled into an affordable apartment of my own. Working the night shift stifled a reasonable social life and wreaked havoc on my schedule. My days off were spent trying to readjust from being a vampire. Occasionally, Travis, a ninth-grader from the church's youth group, would come over to my apartment to play racquetball. Acting like a typical little brother, he thought he knew just what was missing from my life — a man.

the love of God to my siblings, mom, and grandfather. Until then, I will wait!

"So be truly glad. There is wonderful joy ahead, even though you must endure many trials for a little while. These trials will show that your faith is genuine. It is being tested as fire tests and purifies gold, though your faith is far more precious than mere gold. So when your faith remains strong through many trials, it will bring you much praise and glory and honor on the day when Jesus Christ is revealed to the whole world."(1 Peter 1:6-8 NLT)

I was totally unaware that Travis had an agenda. His math teacher, Troy Kessinger, was a Christian bachelor. Travis however, was convinced that we were a perfect match. Personally, I doubted any ninth-graders' definition of the word "perfect." Four months later, in a last ditch effort to get us together, he secretly arranged a blind date.

One evening, in late February, Travis called, "What are you doing Saturday?" It was my weekend off, so I responded, "No plans, do you want to play racquetball?" He quickly answered "No, Troy will pick you up at seven."

My startled brain began running through a zillion "what ifs:" *What if he has facial piercings or a unibrow? What if he smells like a wet dog or has horrible body odor? What if this guy is a weirdo, or even worse, a serial killer?* Following my mini-meltdown, I began to pray. I needed to trust that God would protect me. Reminding myself that this could be an opportunity to make a new guy friend.

It was Saturday afternoon when Troy finally called to confirm plans for the evening. We would eat at Chi Chi's Mexican Restaurant and head downtown to Sax Theater, a Christian comedy club. I was a nervous wreck. While getting ready, I heard a voice calmly say, *"Christon, relax, this is the one."* Ignoring the insanity, I went to the bathroom to check my hair and makeup for the hundredth time. As I stood in front of the mirror, I heard the same voice say, *"Relax, this is the man you are going to marry."* This time, I took a deep breath, forcing myself to say the words out loud, which sounded even crazier. Moments later the doorbell rang and there, standing in front of me, was my husband. I wanted to blurt out, *"Where have you been?*

I have been praying for you for six long years!"

We instantly connected over our passion for Christian music, sharing our favorite songs and artists. After dinner, we drove downtown and sat on a park bench chatting while we waited for the comedy club to open. Our conversation flowed so easily, jumping from one subject to the next. Standing at the ticket window, Troy realized he didn't have his wallet. We retraced our steps, even returning to the restaurant, but the wallet was gone. Taking it all in stride, he asked if I would like to go back to his place to meet his roommate and his black Labrador retriever.

After a quick introduction to his roommate and a belly rub to his creatively named canine, Girl Dog, Troy grabbed his Walkman and a few cassette tapes, escorting me to a hammock outside. The first song he played was called "Look Me In The Eye" by an artist I was unfamiliar with, Margaret Becker. There was a passion in her rich voice and truth in the lyrics that expressed everything I wanted for my life. Wiping the tears away, a little embarrassed, I looked over at Troy and he was crying too. Hours passed as we listened to Christian music with his head at one end of the hammock and mine at the other. *God, please don't let this night end*, I prayed.

There was no question that we both wanted to spend more time together. Our seven year age difference was a breath of fresh air for me because he wasn't trying to find himself or God. He was secure, mature, and honest to his core. He was gentle but strong, witty but sincere, quiet but talkative, intelligent and handsome. My only complaint was that after two months of dating he still had not kissed me. I probably looked ridiculously desperate as I leaned in with lips quivering in anticipation at the end of every date.

Our first trip together was to Panama City to meet my family. Over the last few months, if Troy asked questions about my childhood, I answered truthfully but did not reveal too many details, in fear that he would run away. My anxiety raged as we drove and I prayed, *God, please make them behave.* We were invited to Uncle Bo's for a cookout and my goal was to arrive as early as possible before alcohol consumption levels were too high. When we pulled up to the house at six-thirty, I knew immediately from the amount of cars that this was not a family dinner to meet Chris' new man. This was one of Uncle Bo's Saturday night parties and it had been rocking all afternoon.

The people inside, many of whom I didn't know, were hammered. To my complete embarrassment, my tipsy mother made a big deal announcing our arrival and introducing Troy. Instead of being angry, I chose to just laugh at the irony of these circumstances. Just like I thought, this "cookout" was not for the family to meet Troy, nor was it for us to have dinner together since scraps were all that remained. Other than one drunk gentleman who hung on Troy, repeatedly calling him Darren, despite corrections, no one really noticed we were there.

On our drive back to Orlando, I was unusually quiet. A train wreck emotionally, I tried my best to suppress the barrage of negative self-talk swirling inside of me. I was silently cursing myself for bringing Troy home to meet my family and for the unrealistic expectation that they would have self-control. Convinced that it was just a matter of time before Troy would break up with me, I began imagining the cliches he might use: "You're a really nice girl, but I think we should just be friends," he may say gently. Maybe he would blame it on spiritual improvement, saying, "It's not you, I need to work on my relationship with Jesus." He may choose to rip the bandaid off and say, "I just don't think this is gonna work out, your family is psycho."

I was startled back to reality by Troy's voice, saying, "There is a lot going on in that brain of yours. Do you want to share?"

Immediately, I thought, *This is it, it's over!* Tears streamed down my face as I tried to convey the humiliation I felt.

He pulled the car over, grabbed my hands, looked into my tear-filled eyes, and said, "Christon, you are a miracle. What I saw back there shows me how much God loves you! I love you more now than I did before."

In July, after dating for five months, we took another trip. This time to Black Mountain, North Carolina. Mark, a friend of Troys' from high school, worked in the area at a youth camp. Upon his recommendation, we hiked a beautiful trail by Montreat College called Lookout Mountain Trail. Reaching the top of the mountain, we sat on a large rock enjoying the fresh air and breathtaking views.

"I'll be right back," Troy said rather abruptly. *He must have to use the bathroom,* I thought to myself. When the yellow flies began biting me and there was no sign of him for over fifteen minutes, I began to worry. *Did he get hurt or lost? Would I remember my way back down the trail?* Thankfully, a few moments later, I heard footsteps and was delighted to see Troy reappear through the trees.

When he was close enough to hear me, I frantically asked, "Where have you been?" One of his arms was tucked behind his back. "Are you hurt?" I asked, concerned.

He collapsed to one knee, and breathlessly said, "There are no flowers on this entire mountain. This is all I could find." Pulling his arm forward, he handed me a bundle of different colored leaves and sweetly asked, "Will you marry me?"

No doubts or hesitations this time, it was an absolute, "YES, YES, YES!"

Troy and I attended a few weddings during our courtship, however, neither of us had ever verbalized our personal preferences in a wedding. He had been a groomsman in many large weddings and I wondered if this was his expectation. Selfishly, I wanted something more intimate and romantic, preferably with none of my family present. I imagined a classy white dress, beautiful flowers, and a photographer to capture every detail. All that truly mattered to me was being present with the man I loved, with no distractions. I was surprised to see the look of relief on Troy's face when I shared my dream wedding. Simple and private was his dream too.

On November 6, 1993, a little over eight months from our first date, we were married barefoot on Sunset Beach in St. Petersburg, Florida. I wore a tea length Laura Ashley gown and carried a bouquet made from the dried leaves Troy had given me on Look Out Mountain. In order to prevent hurt feelings, our wedding date remained unannounced, even to our parents. There were only seven people present: Poker and his wife Julie were there as our spiritual mentors and to officiate; Troy's younger brother Chris and wife Missy were our witnesses; two of our friends were there to video and get extra action shots while the professional photographer snapped every precious moment. Ironically, the wedding photographer we hired had never shot a wedding. His expertise was aerial photography. The most thoughtful gift we received was from Poker. He had spliced the amateur videos taken at our wedding and put it to our song - "Say Once More" by Amy Grant. Our wedding was indeed intimate, romantic, and simply perfect.

When we returned to our hotel room that evening we called our close friends and parents to let them know we were married. There were a few hurt feelings but overall everyone was very supportive. I placed my gift to Troy on the bed alongside my pretty nightgown. The gift was the notebook of letters and prayers I had written to my future husband. The last letter in the book was addressed to Troy. He was deeply moved as he flipped through the pages, however, his eyes kept darting over to my nightgown. "Do I have to read this whole book tonight?" he asked sheepishly.

"Yes, every word," I giggled sarcastically, grabbing the nightie and heading to the bathroom to change.

> *To: Troy*
> *From: Christon*
> *November 1993*
> *You are all and so much more than what I have prayed for the last six years. When you stood in my doorway on our first date I was overwhelmed by God's answer to my prayers. I am so undeserving of this blessing. For years I have had to navigate my faith and this world on my own. Not anymore! This new chapter of life is so exciting. We make a great team. I pray that we will make a difference in His Kingdom. Forever Yours.*

To: God
From: Christon
November 1993
Thank you for saving and forgiving me from so many poor choices. I now see that many times when I felt rejection, it was your protection. Thank you for surprising me with a man I didn't know existed. Please help me be the wife Troy needs. (Proverbs 12:4) I want to be his biggest supporter, a faithful listener, and an honest communicator. May he always look forward to coming home.
Forever Yours.

Troy and Christon

Troy, Travis and Christon

Christon - Lookout Mountain

Mr. and Mrs. Kessinger

we thought you'd be here

Wes King

When we got married, Troy was thirty-one years old and many of his friends were on their second child. This did not set off any alarms that our biological clocks were on the brink of extinction. Our motto was simply, "If it happens, it happens." In the meantime, we worked, traveled, remodeled our home, and enjoyed every second as husband and wife.

Two years later our friends and family, even complete strangers, began asking when we planned on having children. Troy coached football and basketball at the high school where he taught math. One evening as we leisurely walked the aisles of Target, a coach who worked with Troy stopped us to chat. Having no filter, he asked when we were going to start making our own football players. This coach then gave us a ten-minute tactless dissertation on the sexual positions that would assure our chances of conceiving a baby. *Seriously, what is wrong with people?* Every time I turned around there was another baby shower to attend or a baby announcement in the mail. Although we weren't actually trying, we weren't preventing it either. This wasn't a topic that was easy to share with my girlfriends. I didn't want them to feel guilty if they got pregnant and hide this special blessing from me out of pity. No one seemed to have trouble getting pregnant, but me.

Tonight, while taking a shower, I was talking to God about my lack of faith in His timing for us to have a baby. We have been married almost two years and I am still not pregnant. As hard as it is for me to understand, I do know that His timing is best. I asked Him tonight for direction on what avenue to take: fertility testing, adoption, or patience. I also asked for His peace and confirmation that He is in control. I trust if there is something medically preventing either of us from having children, God is fully capable of healing.

Getting out of the shower, still talking to God, Habakkuk 2:3 popped into my mind. I was so confused. Is that a book in the Bible? If so, is that strange name a city or a man? I needed help with pronunciation. Did I hear a reference to that name at the women's conference I just attended? I even dared to blame the Devil for tempting me. Quickly I realized that reading my Bible was the last thing the Devil would want. Grumbling as I walked to get my Bible, I thought about the likelihood that these verses would mean nothing. They would probably be some random historical genealogy. I'm sure God wanted to shake me and say, "Just open your Bible!"

Sure enough, Habakkuk was a book and a man in the Old Testament. When I opened Chapter 2, it said in bold print, **The Lord's Answer.** *Immediately overwhelmed, I continued reading: "Then the Lord said to me, write my answer plainly on tablets, so that a runner can carry the correct message to others. This vision is for a future time. It describes the end, and it will be fulfilled. If it seems slow in coming, wait patiently, for it will surely take place. It will not be delayed." (NLT)*

Lord, sometimes I hear you speaking to me and I ignore it thinking it must be my imagination. Help me to be able to distinguish your voice from any others without all the complaining and doubting. I desire to hear from you and act on what you say. As I lay here wet, naked, and sobbing, I want to thank you for loving me. Thank you for answering my prayers tonight. I will write this revelation down and I will wait for it.

We waited patiently for God's promise for months, feeling confident that we were right where God wanted us. However, when the months turned into years the struggle became unbearable. At my yearly female exam, I confided these concerns to the gynecologist.

My Journal:
May 1997
Lord, please help me. Am I taking things into my own hands if we get these two fertility tests? I want to trust you and not get in the way of your plans. Troy is not thrilled about spending money on this, he thinks we need to just have faith. I know that "anyone who trusts in you will never be disgraced." (Romans 9:33 NLT)

Troy and I agreed to the gynecologist's recommendations for some basic non-invasive testing. When the results of those tests were all normal, we decided to proceed to the next phase which included a low-dose oral fertility medication called Clomid. Three months later and still not pregnant, we added another hormone that had to be given intramuscularly. Troy took great delight administering these injections into my derriere. Not only did these medications magnify my emotions but they built up a false hope and expectation each month, leaving me devastated when my menstrual cycle started.

My Journal:
November 1998
Lord, please help me know how to move forward. This fertility medicine makes me sick and overly emotional. The money we have spent so far seems to taunt and hurt me when I am not pregnant at the end of a cycle. I only want to do things your way. Please speak to me.
Thank you for my devotion tonight, You knew exactly what I needed to hear. Here are a few verses from Isaiah 46:3-4, 9-10, 11-12 that really stood out to me. "Listen to me, I have carried you since you were born. Yes, I carried you before you were born. I will be your God throughout your lifetime, until your hair is white with age. I made you, and I will care for you. I will carry you along and save you. Remember the things I have done in the past. For I alone

am God! I am God and there is none like me. Only I can tell you the future before it even happens. Everything I plan will come to pass, for I do whatever I wish. I have said what I will do, and I will do it. Listen to me, you stubborn people."
(NLT)

Forgive me for not listening. Forgive me for not trusting. Forgive me for being stubborn. You have carried me faithfully for twenty-eight years. Why do I doubt you now? I am humbled by your love for me.

This sparked a new fire within me to find joy and purpose in the waiting. The last five years had left me emotionally bankrupt from obsessing over circumstances I could not control. Scouring the scriptures for hope, I was surprised to find so many women just like me. Women like Sarah, Rebekah, Rachel, Hannah, Samson's mother, and Elizabeth. My heart was comforted to see that God heard these women's cries and opened their wombs despite their age, lack of faith, or poor choices. God faithfully answered their prayers and made His name famous in each of their families. My womb was empty now, but God had promised me from the verses in Habbakuk and Isaiah that, "It will be fulfilled. If it seems slow in coming, wait patiently. It will surely take place and will not be delayed. I, God, have said what I will do, and I will do it. Listen to me."

Troy was a balm for my soul, even if we could not have a baby. For the first time in my life I felt stability. There was no drama, unless the phone rang. My mother would call venting about my sister or brother being out of control, or my siblings would call tattling on my mother's excessive drinking. Sadly, I could see that so much of their juvenile issues were directly connected to my mother's inability to discipline or guide them while inebriated. Confronting my mother's alcohol addiction made her defensive, putting an awkward wedge in our relationship. I prayed fervently that she would stop finding comfort in a substance. Troy spoke truth to my anxious heart in these moments, reminding me that it wasn't in my job description to open a womb or save my family, these tasks belonged to God.

As the holidays approached I decided it was time to pause all fertility medications. My hormones needed a reset and mental clarity usually came when I retreated to my journal. Since the third grade, when gifted a diary with a little lock, writing had been a safe place for me to process life. After becoming a Christian, it was also where I wrote lessons the Lord was teaching me. *Returning to these journals, it is obvious that I am a slow learner.*

> *My Journal:*
> *April 1999*
> *I read the story of Rachel and Leah today in Genesis chapters 20-30. Major drama when two sisters are married to the same man. It dawned on me that both women were "empty," struggling with the 'if I had' disease. Rachel's womb was empty, leaving her to think, 'if I had' a baby my life would be whole. Leah had an empty heart, thinking, 'if I had' a man who loved me I would be whole. Life would be better 'if I just had' this or that. For years, I too thought 'if I had' a father who was present, a mother who was healthy, friends who loved Jesus, a Christian boyfriend, money for college or a car, then life would be great.*
>
> *Lord, I have contracted this disease again, thinking 'if I had' a baby then I would be content. The truth is, I have never felt whole or complete unless there was Jesus. Thankful for the reminder that only you can fill my empty places.*

At the beginning of June, Troy and I packed the car and drove out west for eighteen days. We camped and hiked all over Yellowstone, Bryce Canyon, Zion National Park, and the Grand Canyon. Life was good, just the two of us. Our eight-month fast from fertility medications and procedures had been a blessing, refocusing us on the things that were important.

On our drive back to Florida, Troy revealed he had been praying about the direction we should take in starting a family. He was open to one more round of fertility injections, and if that was unsuccessful, he would like to begin exploring adoption. This was huge! Up to this point, I felt like he was never really on board with the fertility plan. Honestly, at times I probably coerced or manipulated him to cooperate.

My Journal:
1 July 1999
*I called Dr. Loy's office today and spoke with his nurse. She
is excited that we will be starting another round of Clomid
with the injections. I told her that I felt bloated with some
mild cramping, and would likely start my menstrual cycle
any minute. It is the 4th of July weekend so their office is
closed on Monday. She set my appointment for Tuesday
morning where I will get blood work which will include
a pregnancy test, and an ultrasound. Depending on those
results, injections will start that evening. Lord, you are in
control, I trust you.*

That same Friday, I was surprised to see my mother
spontaneously show up on our doorstep. This was exactly what my
anxious heart needed to get me through the weekend. The trip to
our home was a much needed reset for her too. The last year had
been traumatic, her best friend who was also a co-worker, neighbor
and drinking buddy, passed away quickly from pancreatic cancer.
This devastating loss, in combination with her own medical scare,
was the catalyst that broke her ten-year addiction to alcohol. I was
so proud of this woman! Her contagious laughter, creativity, and
selfless spirit had resurfaced. That weekend, we stayed busy with
house projects, cooking, and a 4th of July celebration with Troy's
family. Nervousness and fear escalated as each day crept closer to my
doctor's appointment.

My Journal:
4 July 1999
*The sermon at church today was about God being the
creator. The pastor emphasized that when we get down about
our current circumstances, God gently places his hand on us
and says, "Have faith, remember I can make something out of
nothing." Troy elbowed me and said "He looked right at you
when he said that."*

On the drive to Dr. Loy's office Tuesday morning, my mother
prayed out loud, "Lord, please make something out of nothing."

Because I had not started my menstrual cycle, the doctor decided to hold off on the ultrasound. Labs which included a pregnancy test were drawn and I was instructed that a nurse would call later in the day with the results. In order to keep my mind in a healthy space, I turned on loud worship music while my mother and I cleaned and painted the inside of our garage. At three o'clock, covered in blue paint, my mind began to unravel. I convinced myself that the nurse must be waiting to call the patients with bad news at the end of the day. After a hot shower with lots of tears, the phone rang. *Christon, this is the nurse from Dr. Loy's office. Honey, you are pregnant!*

There were no words, just laughter and tears. I was reminded of the verse where Sarah says, "God has brought me laughter. All who hear about this will laugh with me." (Genesis 21:6 NLT) Clearly, God had opened my womb. There was no doctor or drug that would get the glory. His name would be the only one we praised! To our absolute delight and overwhelming gratitude, Elijah Thomas Kessinger was born on February 26, 2000.

All-State Quarterback 2018

Introducing Team Kessingers newest star!

Coaches Troy and Christon Kessinger signed this future hall of famer, Elijah Thomas Kessinger, to their team on February 26, 2000. This 7 lb. 2 oz. future star came in at 19.5" and is already a dominant force on the Kessinger squad.

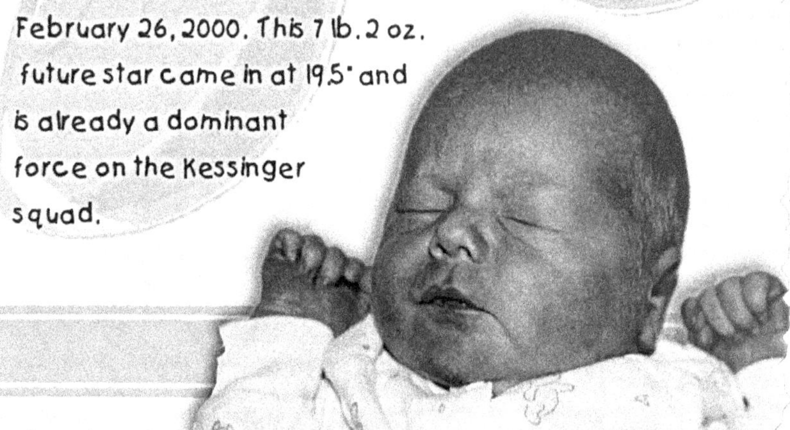

Eli Thomas Kessinger - 2000

the great adventure

Steven Curtis Chapman

I had no desire to be a stay-at-home mom until I became Eli's mommy. Every time I left him with the sitter I was a wreck. I loved being home with him and selfishly didn't want to miss a single burp or giggle. Troy and I discussed our options however, it was not feasible financially for me to even cut back to part-time. The cost of living in Orlando was just too high. So, I tattled to God.

> *My Journal:*
> *December 2001*
> *This is what I prayed in the shower tonight:*
> *Lord, I need to turn this whole "staying home" thing over*
> *to you. You decide if it is important or if working outside*
> *the home is where you want me to be. I would hate to be*
> *whining about something that I am not even sure I would*
> *like. What if I hated being at home all the time? What if I*
> *couldn't handle the cut in our income? Troy says that we*
> *would have to sell our home and move into a trailer. I trust*
> *you to work out the details and change Troy's heart if me*
> *staying home is what is best for our family.*

On January 1, 2002 we received a random call from one of Troy's close friends telling him about a head football position open in another state. The timing of this phone call was an absolute God moment. I sat there stunned. Troy had no idea what I had been praying and his friend was totally clueless. Although we did not pursue the job, God was obviously stirring something inside of Troy. A few days later he said, "Christon, I want you to be at home with Eli. Are you ready for a big change? What do you think about Georgia?"

Over the next five months, Troy sent resumes to fifteen high schools in Georgia and North Carolina. There were a few interviews but nothing came of them. Naturally, when May rolled around we both recognized that the door must have closed in this area, at least for this year. Most head football positions would have been filled before May, enabling the coach to be on campus for spring conditioning. *Note to self, when you think things are impossible, that is usually when God shows up.*

> *My Journal:*
> *20 May 2002*
> *Oh Lord, the fun roller coaster of life! Troy's best friend Bob called tonight from North Carolina. A member of his church is a new principal at one of the local high schools. He just happened to mention to Bob at lunch today that he needs a Geometry teacher (Troy's expertise) and a head football coach. Seriously? Troy is flying up there this week for an interview.*

Let me clarify here that no one in our family or friend group knew we were discussing the possibility of a move or of Troy applying to be a head football coach. We recognized that these phone calls were not coincidences, but sweet nudges from the Lord. He saw us, heard us, and was working on our behalf.

One of Troy's greatest qualities is his unwavering faith. There is no worrying about the details of a situation or fretting when God places him in a waiting room. He simply trusts that God will do what only He can do. I have often been frustrated that I was not wired more like Troy. *Why did I always seem to question God or throw a tantrum when I had to wait? I should be thankful that I have had ample opportunities to grow in this area over the years, resulting in a very active prayer life.*

A week following Troy's interview in North Carolina, we received the disappointing news that the head football coach position was given to another candidate. I was confused, it felt so right. The unexpected way everything fell into place appeared to be God's hand. I had to trust that God was in control, praying that He would place our family right where we needed to be. The following day, in the middle of my questioning, the principal called again. He asked Troy if he was still interested in the position, their first choice was unhirable. Although Troy may not have been the principal's first choice, he was who God had chosen.

We were off on a new adventure to Southport, North Carolina. There were so many mixed emotions about moving away from what was comfortable and familiar, but we both yearned for a more simple life. Waving goodbye to the rat race of Orlando in hopes of making a difference in a small town was a dream that had now become a reality. I prayed for wisdom in my new role as a stay-at-home mom, hoping I would be productive, supportive, creative, and content.

My Journal:
November 2002
Eli is now 21 months old and is such a chatterbox. The three of us drove to Wilmington tonight. Every time Troy and I started a conversation, Eli interrupted, saying, "Mommy, Mommy." When we stopped talking, he would quickly think of something to say like, "Where are we going?" It became frustrating as he repeatedly interrupted with nothing significant to report. Finally, I said, "Eli, if you don't have anything important to say, please just listen to the music and let Mommy and Daddy talk." Thirty seconds into our next conversation, Eli said, "Mommy, Mommy." Sarcastically, I responded "Yes, Eli." He blurted out, "Do you have a baby in your tummy?" Troy and I looked at each other baffled and confused. Why in the world would he ask that question? Eli proceeded to say, "When Santa comes you will have a baby in your tummy." Troy laughed, saying "Is he a little prophet?"

A few days after Christmas, I began having lower pelvic pain and nausea. We had plans to go out of town and I was concerned that I may have a stomach virus. Feeling a little silly, I bought a home pregnancy test, remembering Eli's prediction about me being pregnant at Christmas. We were stunned when it turned positive immediately! Eli was right, there was a baby in my tummy when Santa came.

As we entered 2003, we had so much to be thankful for: Troy loved his new job, I was thriving as a stay-home mom, we were plugged into a small church with amazing new friends, and we were overjoyed to have another baby on the way. According to the book *What to Expect When You're Expecting*, the baby and I were meeting all of our milestones, until we entered the third trimester. I began having mild spotting and contractions which the OB/GYN thought was a result of overdoing it and dehydration. When light duty and forcing fluids were unsuccessful, I was admitted to the hospital.

Initially, the hydration fluids decreased the contractions and the bleeding had ceased, giving us hope that a discharge was imminent. Unfortunately, on my fourth night in the hospital, I woke up covered in blood. Immediately I was transferred to the Maternity Intensive Care Unit where I was attached to monitors, given steroid injections for the baby's lungs, and a battery of tests were performed. We were told that I had placenta previa, a condition where the placenta pulls away from the lining of the uterus. The duration of this pregnancy would be spent in the hospital on strict bed rest.

My Journal:
22 July 2003
I am back to waiting and worrying Lord. Being out of control, slowing down and listening, do not come easy for me… but here I am. Help me to trust, rest, and hear the lessons you want to teach me during this pause in my life.

How appropriate that this was the verse in my devotion today: "Therefore, my beloved sister, be steadfast, **immovable***, always abounding in the work of the Lord, knowing that in the Lord your* **labor** *is not in vain." (1 Corinthians 15:58 ESV)*

The hospital was a forty-minute drive from our home so the weekly hugs and kisses from Troy and Eli were priceless, a lifeline to my lonely soul. Selfishly, I wished the boys could visit more, however, logically I realized this was a critical time of year for Troy as a head football coach. I also wanted my mommy, but my demanding grandfather, Poppi, needed her more at the moment. There was comfort knowing that her bags were packed, ready to come the minute I went into labor. For the time being, we were in good hands and her daily calls of encouragement would have to suffice.

People in our community showered our family for five weeks with the most thoughtful acts of service. Countless meals were sent to our home and friends rotated watching Eli while Troy worked. I was spoiled with surprise visits from friends, church members, and even a few of Troy's co-workers. They brought me books and magazines to read, homemade meals and desserts, baby gifts, music, and I was even treated to a pedicure.

It became quite apparent that it wasn't just the baby that needed me to be still. I continued to hear a gentle whisper reminding me to *listen*. Each morning after the doctors had done their rounds, I would pull out my journal and Bible, asking God to speak to me. Up to this point in my faith journey I had spent very little time in the Old Testament, so it was super weird when I felt a nudge to open the book of Isaiah. I was shaken when Isaiah used the word *listen* six times in the first chapter, sealing the place in the Bible where He wanted me to camp out. As the weeks on bedrest passed, it was the prophet Isaiah's words that comforted me. The lessons I learned during my hospital lockdown with Jesus, would end up filling an entire journal. Here are just a few:

My Journal:
Summer 2003
Lessons from God's waiting room:

1. *When I complained and whined about why I was stuck in a hospital feeling completely out of control it was the words, "Why do you complain and say my way is hidden from the Lord; my cause is disregarded by my God? Do you not know? Have you not heard? The Lord is the everlasting God, the Creator of the ends of the earth. He will not grow tired or weary and his understanding no one can fathom." (Isaiah 40:27-28 NIV)*

2. *When my body ached all over not just from being pregnant but from lack of movement, it was the words, "He gives strength to the weary and increases the power of the weak." (Isaiah 40:29 NIV)*

3. *When my contractions were out of control, blood covered my body, and I was scared for the future of my unborn child, it was the words, "Do not fear for I am with you; do not be dismayed, for I am your God. I will strengthen you and help you; I will uphold you with my righteous right hand." (Isaiah 41:10 NIV)*

4. *When guilt swept over me for the burdens I felt like I had placed on my husband and others, it was the words, "The Lord longs to be gracious to you; He rises to show you compassion." (Isaiah 30:18 NIV)*

5. *When I felt forgotten and alone in my hospital bed, it was the words, "Can a mother forget the baby at her breast and have no compassion on the child she has borne? Though she may forget, I will not forget you! See, I have engraved you on the palms of my hands." (Isaiah 49:15-16 NIV)*

I praise your name for opening my womb and allowing Troy and I to be parents. (Isaiah 54:1 NIV) Please pour out your Spirit on our offspring and your blessings on our descendants. I pray that our children will grow up to be strong like poplar trees and able to say, "I belong to the Lord." (Isaiah 44:3-5 NIV) Please give Troy and I wisdom to guide and direct our children to you. "All your sons will be taught by the Lord and great will be their peace." (Isaiah 54:13 NIV)

Three weeks before my due date, the obstetrician felt like
the baby's lungs were developed enough to schedule induction. The
wait was finally over. On August 12, 2003, we celebrated the birth
of a healthy baby boy, Samuel McKee Kessinger. My mother, who
Eli had named Gammoo, arrived at the hospital a few hours before
our discharge bearing gifts. One was a light blue t-shirt for Eli
announcing, "I'm the Big Brother," which he proudly slipped over his
head. The other gift was a cozy preemie onesie she had bought for
Sammy's trip home. Eli eagerly volunteered to be Gammoo's helper
as she changed the baby. That is, until he saw "the worm." Grossed
out by the two-inch freshly cut umbilical cord hanging from his
brother's belly, he withdrew all further services.

I was not prepared for juggling life with an active toddler
and a breastfeeding infant. The time commitment of being a head
football coach kept Troy consumed with work, especially during
the fall semester. I wanted to be a supportive coach's wife and have
dinner ready when he walked through the door, but this was totally
unrealistic. To be honest, I was exhasted and struggled to find our
new normal.

My Journal:
7 June 2004
*Not sure what we were thinking when we decided to take a
four-year-old and a ten-month-old camping in Vermont. Eli
has fought sleep since he was an infant. Putting him to bed
is an exhausting chore. Here are his many excuses for not
wanting to sleep: I am thirsty, I need to go potty, I need my
toy, I need the door cracked, I need more hugs and kisses,
I didn't say "night night don't let the bugs bite," I am just
not sleepy, I am scared of the dark, or the best one - I forgot
to say "night night to the rugs." Bedtime is taxing enough
when we are home, but when we are on vacation with all
four of us sleeping in one room, it is torture! I am so grumpy.*

Two days before Sammy's first birthday I was feeling a little puny and decided to do a home pregnancy test. I collapsed on the bathroom floor weeping when I saw the results. *How could I be pregnant again when I was still breastfeeding Sammy?*

The memories were still fresh from my last pregnancy and thoughts of returning to a hospital for weeks, alone, left me shaken. This time, the tears were not from a place of joy but fear. Trying to hold back my emotions, I called Troy at work, asking him to please come home for lunch. He must have been suspicious, since I never called him at work and a lunch date was not normal for us. When he walked through the door he had a huge smile plastered on his face and blurted out, "You're pregnant!" These words incited a steady stream of tears to cascade down my cheeks. He was confused when he saw my disillusioned face and gently questioned, "You cried for years because you weren't pregnant. Why are you crying now when you are?"

"How will we afford three children on one income?" I cried.

"Honey, if you are worried about how we will afford another child, STOP! This baby is a blessing from God and He will provide everything we need," he consoled.

We loved everything about Southport: The convenience of living two minutes from the high school and ten minutes from the beach, the strong connections we felt in our church, storytime at the local library, game nights with friends, my MOPS group, the quaint shops downtown and our favorite restaurants. We had even completed a beautiful addition to our home. There was only one issue: Troy felt called to leave. After three years of trying to change the trajectory of the football program with little success, he thought someone else might be more successful. He was fortunate to secure a position in his hometown as an assistant coach and teacher at Oviedo High School. It broke my heart to leave but I knew we were doing the right thing. God had been preparing me for a few months in my time alone with Him. We returned to Orlando, clinging to Jesus, praying that it would only be for a season. Troy needed time to reset and I needed to deliver our third baby.

Troy and I made a pact with each pregnancy to be surprised by the baby's gender on their birth-day. This time was different. It wasn't an ultrasound that exposed the gender, it was a promise the Lord gave me in the shower nine months earlier. On March 31, 2005, we held our beautiful, bald, blue-eyed baby girl who Troy named Annie Lee. The first time Eli held his baby sister in the hospital, I heard him whisper, "You're in good hands now."

Staying home with three small children made it difficult to get out or develop new friendships. My days were spent changing diapers, nursing, playing with match box cars, reading children's books, and singing silly songs. The moment my husband walked through the door after a long day of teaching and coaching, ready to relax, I greeted him with thousands of untapped adult words. Little did he know, I had unloaded hundreds of words during naptime when I made long distance calls to my best friend, Tabitha in Southport or my mother in Panama City.

My Journal:
June 2005
I camped out in chapters five and six of Deuteronomy tonight. The Israelites were so ready to enter the Promised Land. I feel their pain as Troy and I both feel unsettled here in Orlando. The pace is so fast and relationships are superficial. Honestly, I feel invisible here. What is your plan Lord? When will we enter our Promised Land?

Jehovah Jireh, you are enough. Help me to be content right here, right now. In Deuteronomy five, you reminded the Israelites to sit tight and obey right where they were until it was time to move. You spoke to them, and I trust that you will speak to me too.

Until the next step is revealed, I am going to snuggle close to you. I know you will deliver us to a new place. A city where we will flourish. You will supply all of our needs. (Philippians 4:19 NIV) You will do more than we could ever dream or imagine. (Ephesians 3:20 NIV) You blew the Israelites' minds when they arrived in the Promised Land and your word says you never change. (Malachi 3:6 NIV) Thank you for preparing the next crazy adventure!

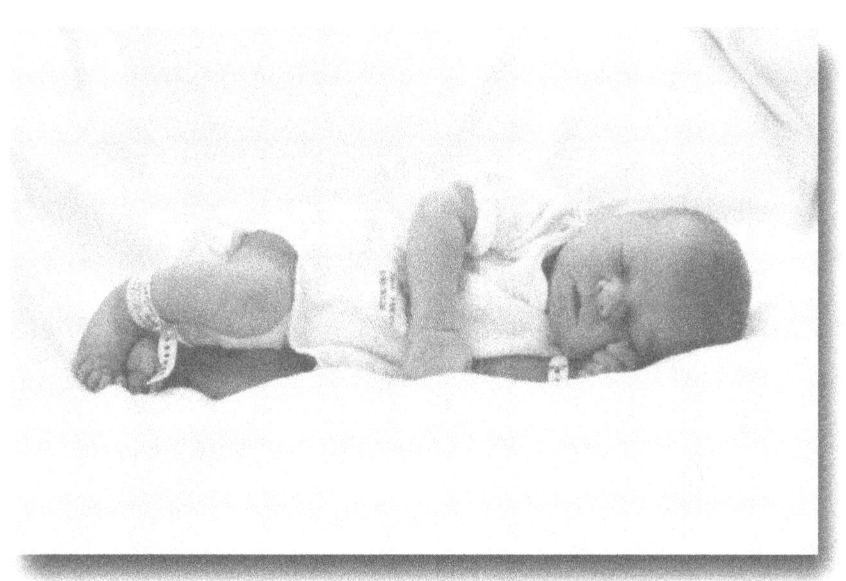

Samuel McKee Kessinger - 2003

Annie Lee Kessinger - 2005

Jadon Lavik

For the next six months our life was on cruise control. Troy had very little stress being an assistant football coach and math teacher at the high school. Eli started kindergarten, which gave me a few hours of free time when Sammy and Annie napped. We also had the added blessing of my mother-in-law, Soni, living a few miles away.

One evening, after the children were tucked into bed, Troy asked if I would pick up a For Sale By Owner sign the next time I went to Walmart. This wasn't a surprise since we both had been praying about our next step. Actually, I had been waiting for the green light. Let's go!

My Journal:
6 March 2006
Lord, there are so many unknowns for our family right now. We blindly put a For Sale sign in our front yard today. Where will you send us? You know our heart's desire is to live in a small affordable town. A safe place to raise our children where we can be involved in our community and make your name famous.

Caught myself asking a bunch of "what ifs" tonight. Troy redirected me by saying, "Christon, you must move away from all the 'what ifs' and focus on the 'whens/wins.'

Our home was on the market for two weeks when Troy
received an unexpected phone call from a coach he had known for
many years. This coach had been offered a job at a Christian private
school in South Carolina. The timing was not right to move his
family, but he immediately thought of Troy.

My Journal:
23 March 2006
*We did not recognize the out-of-town number tonight on the
caller ID and almost ignored it. I am laying on the couch
giggling my head off as I hear Troy talk with Coach Flath:
"Well, Coach, your timing can't be more perfect. My wife
and I just put our house on the market a few days ago. We
told God we were available and you called. I won't say no if
this is from Him."*

*Troy immediately sent his resume to the email address
Coach Flath had provided and within fifteen minutes
the Headmaster called. Amazing God, only you could
orchestrate circumstances like this. Clearly, this is so we will
say, "Look what God did!"*

Eight days later, Troy had accepted the position as head
football coach, athletic director, and high school math teacher
at Thomas Sumter Academy. The school was located in Sumter,
South Carolina, and educated students from kindergarten through
twelfth grade. The board's vote was unanimous and the offer was so
humbling that Troy and I fell to the floor crying, thanking God over
and over for His faithfulness.

We decided that I would stay back with the children until
the house was sold. There were a zillion things that needed to be
accomplished before he left. On the top of the list was making Troy
an appointment for a vasectomy before our insurance changed.
Unfortunately, we were turned away at the visit saying we needed a
referral from our primary doctor. There simply wasn't enough time.

The children all reacted differently to their daddy being gone for two months. Annie Lee was just learning how to talk, and many times when a man passed us in the grocery store, she pointed at him, declaring, "Da Da." Sammy had been a great sleeper, but recently he refused to even lay down, saying, "I'm waiting on Daddy to come home." Eli, who was six years old, tried to be a big boy. "Mommy, if you ever need help spanking the children, I can do that, cause when you spank it doesn't hurt."

I desperately wanted to fix our situation which led me to overthink everything. My "what ifs" were out of control.

nothing compared to what I am going to do." I continued to read verses 19-22. Unbelievable! Paraphrased, it said, "I am about to do a new thing. Don't you see it? I will make a way for your family and someday you will honor me before the whole world. Just ask for my help." So on my knees, wrapped in a towel, sobbing, I begged God to intervene.

That summer, our Florida neighbors took turns mowing our grass weekly and serving our family in numerous other ways. In Sumter, Troy was blessed by people in the community inviting him to dinner and giving him free lodging. Then on July 17th, the head coach for the middle school football team, Horace Scott, pulled Troy aside and said, "My wife, Kathy, and I have a lake house about fifty minutes from the school. We want your family to be together." As he handed Troy the keys, he said, "You can stay in it, rent free, as long as you need it."

My Journal:
20 July 2006
I am humbled and overwhelmed by God's goodness to us the last two weeks. So many people, even strangers, have been generous to our family. I have been praying that God would show us how we can reciprocate that same generosity. As I was packing tonight, I received a phone call from our realtor. There was a prayer request in her church's bulletin about a young missionary couple in need of a place to stay as they attended seminary in the area. For some reason, God told her to call us. They are coming tomorrow to check it out. So God!

Just days after arriving at the lake house, while we were still trying to unpack and organize, Troy received a phone call from our close friend and pastor in Southport, NC. He was concerned about a former football player Troy had coached two years earlier. This player, Josh, was now a high school senior. His parents were engulfed in a bitter divorce battle and his love for football was squelched by a foul mouthed head coach he did not respect. Josh was dreading his senior year, voicing his ultimate wish, to play football for Coach

Kessinger. Initially, this was not about us housing him. There was angst about the perception that it might look like Troy was recruiting players, which was frowned upon. When Troy came to me about the situation, I adamantly opposed Josh living with someone we did not know. If this young man was coming to Thomas Sumter Academy, there would only be one family he lived with, and that would be us.

My Journal:
23 August 2006
We have a new addition to our family, Josh. He is a seventeen-year-old who Troy coached at South Brunswick a few years ago. People think we are totally crazy to bring a teenager we don't know well into our home. Not to mention, the home isn't ours and we have only lived in it a few days. Many have dared to ask, "Aren't you concerned about the safety of your three children and the negative influences an adolescent might expose them to?" Yep, it would be so easy to jump down the "what if" rabbit hole once again, however, this time I prayed first and I have peace about this situation. I am not naive and do realize that being a guardian to someone else's child is a tremendous responsibility!

Lord, give us the wisdom and resources we need to guide and direct this teenage boy. May we be found faithful in your eyes. We are holding to your promise in James 1:5, "If you need wisdom, ask our generous God, and he will give it to you. He will not rebuke you for asking." (NLT)

To our delight, Josh loved our children. He slid into his new role as their adopted big brother without missing a beat. Our biggest challenge with this six-foot-two, two-hundred and eighty-five pound teenager living under our roof, was keeping his belly full. This was often fulfilled by the gallons of milk he drank weekly.

Prior to writing this chapter, I would have told you the lessons from this season of our lives revolved mostly around my husband being a role model for Josh, showing him how to be a Godly man, husband, and father. However, after reading my journals, I see God's hand all over the lessons He needed to teach me. The most important lesson was to trust Him. At the time, I was mentally consumed with our financial status and an assortment of "what ifs" surrounding our unsold Florida home. In hindsight, it is crazy that instead of relieving any of these burdens, God added another one, a teenager. In His perfect wisdom the distraction of Josh's presence in our lives gave me daily opportunities to serve and get my eyes off of our current circumstances. These were things I had no control of anyway. It was important that Josh live in a stable home, exposed to a couple that genuinely believed God would show up.

The six of us lived in the two-bedroom lake house for eight months when an opportunity to move into an unoccupied church parsonage presented itself. The parsonage was built in 1930 and had a large red tin roof, which the children cleverly nicknamed the Red Roof House. Although it was much bigger than we needed, it was a blessing for our family in so many ways. For one, it was a ten-minute drive to the school, saving Troy an hour and forty-five minutes each day. Money was extremely tight and after tithing, paying bills, and buying groceries, twenty-nine dollars remained in our bank account each month. To add a rental payment to our already stretched budget could have been a deal breaker, however, the amount was exactly what we were already paying in gas to and from the lake house. Huge blessing!

Nothing we did fell into what the world deemed as the appropriate order. What most people did not know is that we were not flippantly making decisions, we were praying like crazy. If they peeked into one of my journals, it would be obvious that it was NOT the order I would have chosen, either.

My Journal:
1 March 2007
I am pregnant! Although I am in shock, it is not surprising since I have not taken my birth control pills all month. Oops! This sounds weird, but ever since we were turned away at the urologist office in Orlando, I had this gut feeling that we were not done having children.

I did not handle my last pregnancy very well. I worried the entire nine months about finances, managing a third child, and fear of being hospitalized again. Add to that the stress of moving back to Florida so late in the pregnancy. Lord, I refuse to do that again. Despite numerous uncertainties, you will meet all of our needs and teach us lessons we will never forget. Thank you for this precious life growing inside of me. May we be faithful to raise all four of these children to love and honor you.

Thank goodness the Lord holds his creation together, Colossians 1:17, or we may not have survived the saturation of change in 2007. Not only did people look at us cross-eyed when we announced the news of a fourth Kessinger on the way, but they had serious doubts about our sanity when we bought a five-acre piece of property and signed a contract with a builder. This just didn't make sense, especially when our Florida home was still on the market. As if this was not enough, Troy's mother, Soni, who the children called Mama, wanted to move in with us. She had been living alone in Florida for three years after her husband, Troy's daddy, passed away from mesothelioma. I had hoped her motivation for this big change was to be closer to her grandchildren and not that she sensed her daughter-in-law was on the verge of losing it.

My Journal:
1 December 2007
Lord, I must trust that you know what you are doing. I am exhausted from all the "what ifs" that have flooded my mind for twenty-one months. You know that if we don't sell the house (in Florida) in the next thirty days that our property taxes, yearly association fees, and homeowner's insurance will all be due. The first payment on the property here is due mid-January and construction will begin shortly after. You know that we currently don't have this money. Our circumstances are not hidden from you. If we have found favor in your eyes, PLEASE give us a sign that we are walking in your will. "We hear songs of praise from the ends of the earth, songs that give glory to the Righteous one!" (Isaiah 24:16 NLT)

Today I will choose praise:

•Praise you for rescuing me.

•Praise you for making it possible to get a college education.

•Praise you for answered prayers.

•Praise you that I am married to a man who loves Jesus and me.

•Praise you for opening my womb.

•Praise you for allowing me the opportunity to be a stay-at-home mommy.

•Praise you for delivering a job that Troy loves in a small community.

•Praise you for giving us all we need each month.

*•**WHEN** you sell the Florida home in the next thirty days, people all around will hear our shouts of praise to a God who provides.*

Thinking back to Christmas in the Red Roof House, my heart fills with joy. Although Josh had graduated and moved on to the next chapter of his life, in his place arrived another milk-drinking boy, Benjamin Delano Kessinger. This chunky, laid back little fellow completed our family.

Resources were limited, so presents for the children were provided by two loving grandmothers, Mama and Gammoo. My gift to Troy was a surprise performance of the Nativity put on by our children, featuring Benjamin as baby Jesus swaddled in a laundry basket. *This play would become a family tradition for the next ten years, until baby Jesus (Benjamin) no longer fit in the laundry basket.* Troy made me an origami box out of red and green construction paper with my name sparkling in glitter on the top. Inside were six folded pieces of paper each with a letter on it, spelling out "My Girl." There was a precious love note written inside all six. The creativity, thoughtfulness and time he put into this gift touched my heart more than any purchased gift ever could.

Two days after Christmas, our prayers were answered. The Florida home sold and the money was wired to us on December 30th. Despite my whining, worrying, and "what if-ing" for almost two years, God was right on time. We indeed shouted His praises! To remind us of God's faithfulness, that sweet origami box is the first gift under our tree every Christmas.

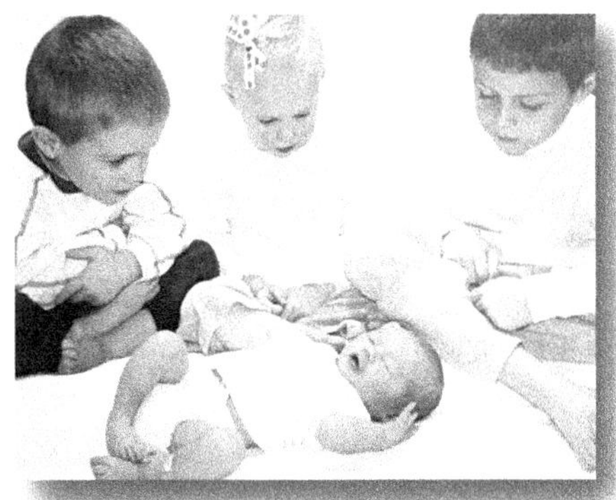

Sammy, Annie & Eli checking out baby brother Benjamin - 2007

Nativity Play - 2007

Origami box

God is Good

CHAPTER 20
angel by your side

Francesca Battistelli

Troy and I have been committed throughout our marriage to have an open door policy. This would include anyone who needed a place to stay or teenagers who needed a safe place to talk about hard things. We did not have spare money to give people, but we could always provide a warm bed or a supportive environment.

> *My Journal:*
> *11 October 2009*
> *Thank you, Lord, for meeting me here this morning. I was touched by your faithfulness when I read Psalm 37:26 "They are always generous and lend freely; their children will be blessed."(NIV) Then the wind blew the pages of my bible to Psalm 41:1"Blessed is he who has regard for the weak; the Lord delivers him in times of trouble."(NIV) The rest of the chapter tells me that you will protect, preserve, bless, sustain, and restore us. I will praise your name forever.*

Over the years, a total of seven people lived with us for a season. Some were family members who needed a reset in their life.

Others were friends or previous students who were in the midst of a crisis and needed healing. Because Troy worked with teens in the classroom and on the football field, it was a perfect gateway for us to have a ministry in our home. Due to my own experiences as a teenager, I longed for young people to grasp that they, too, could have a sweet relationship with Jesus. Many of our closest friends today were former students or players that we had the privilege of mentoring as high school students in our Bible studies.

> *My Journal:*
> *14 September 2010*
> *Last night our high school Bible study was on clinging to Jesus when life throws us a curveball. We challenged the students to not shrink back or be surprised when trials come our way. (1 Peter 4:12-13) I had no idea that I would have to apply these words so soon.*
>
> *My mom called today to tell me that her doctor's office wants her to come in tomorrow to review the results of an abdominal CAT scan she had yesterday. The worry and tension in her voice disturbs me. I do not want her to receive results without someone present. I feel helpless.*
>
> *I called the doctor's office and spoke with the nurse practitioner. I updated her on some of our family history and the concerns I had of my mom being alone for the appointment. She was very understanding and honest about the seriousness of their findings. They want to do a biopsy on her pancreas to rule out pancreatic cancer.*

For ten years my mother had not put a drop of alcohol to her lips. As a result, we talked several times a day. The miles between us drove me bonkers. There was no reason for her to remain in Florida as all of our family had either moved out of the area or had passed away, including her father. The distance also handicapped the relationship my children, now ten, seven, five and three, could have with their grandmother, Gammoo. My need to get her close to me and the children was now exacerbated by her present health issues.

Woke up in a panic this morning from a horrible dream. In the dream, my mother had taken her life because she felt like a burden to her family. Lord, please give her hope to fight whatever battle lies ahead and let her know how much she is loved.

When we spoke on the telephone this afternoon, she began our conversation by asking me this question: "I need you to be honest with me Twink, how are you feeling about the news we have received so far?" She knows that my years of working as a pediatric oncology nurse must give me some perspective. I told her the truth. "I am worried about what the pathology will find but I am choosing to focus on the fun we will have when you get here." Hoping to lift her spirits, I shared a list the children have begun titled, "To Do With Gammoo." Things like draw together, read Halloween books, play baseball in the backyard, and show Gammoo our dog, cat, fish, and hamster are what they have written so far.

Now it was my turn to inquire, "Mom, how are you feeling about all of this?" She skirted the question by telling me a story about a friend. This friend, Rick, had battled esophageal cancer for years. At one point during his treatment he mentioned that he often visualized himself flying his airplane into the side of a mountain so he wouldn't be a burden to his family. My heart sank, recalling my nightmare. I immediately responded, "Mom, I am honored to love and serve you. Please don't rob me of this joy. When people commit suicide, their loved ones are left with so much confusion, regret, and anger. If the tables were turned and I only had ten minutes to live and in those few minutes, I chose to check out early, would that not crush you? Would you not be begging for just ten more minutes?"

Thank you Lord, for giving me a glimpse into her emotional state and preparing me for our conversation. I was encouraged by this verse today, "Don't be afraid of what you are about to suffer. The devil will test you. But if you remain faithful even when facing death, I will give you the crown of life." (Revelation 2:10 NLT)

An endoscopic ultrasound and biopsy were done at the Medical University of South Carolina (MUSC) in Charleston on the twenty-ninth of September. The diagnosis was devastating: inoperable pancreatic cancer. The future was now scary and filled with thousands of questions. Very few words were spoken on the two-hour drive home until my mother broke the silence: "When we get close to your house, pull into a gas station so we can freshen up. Today is Soni's birthday and I don't want this news to taint our celebration tonight. Promise me that no one will know this diagnosis until tomorrow." I honored her request as we plastered artificial smiles on our faces to open gifts, eat cake, and sing Happy Birthday to my mother-in-law. However, when the party was over and everyone was asleep, I climbed into bed with my mother.

My Journal:
30 September 2010
The surgeon said the tumor is worrisome because it is wrapped around major blood vessels at the neck of the pancreas. The chemotherapy and radiation administered will only be palliative. This means it will only shrink the tumor, not eliminate it. All to make her more comfortable.

It was after midnight by the time everyone was tucked in bed and I could not fall asleep. I felt certain that my mother would still be awake, trying to process the news, so I went to her room. Our emotions were raw as we cried and held each other. At one point she said, "I will miss you so much!" When I asked if she was afraid, her response was, "I am not afraid to die, just afraid of the process of it. I don't want my sweet grandbabies to see me deteriorate. There is a weird smell when people are dying and I don't want that to be their last memory of me." Not sure where she concocted that theory, however, I promised to make sure she looked and smelled beautiful as we walked this journey together.

I don't know how much time we have left, but I needed to be certain that we would spend forever together. Boldly I asked, "Mom, I will hold your hand until we reach the door of heaven, but only you can knock on it. Do you have confidence that it will open?" She responded, "Twinkie,

I have made a lot of mistakes and I hope you kids have learned from me what not to do. I know I haven't gone to church as much as I should have, and reading the Bible has always been difficult for me. To be honest, I have trouble understanding it. But, I love the Lord, I know He forgives me, and I talk to Him every day."

Lord, I know you see my breaking heart. Thank you for giving me a peace tonight about where my mom's forever home will be, however, I'm not ready for her to go there yet.

On occasion, my mother would tell me she was praying for something specific for one of us, but for the most part, her faith had always been private. The brevity of life gave her a new confidence to ask questions and talk more openly about the Lord. *When I began going through her journals many years later, it was touching to see the prayers she had written for the people she loved. In Chapter 3, I mentioned her 1981 New Year's Resolutions where she wrote - "Hopefully I'll be a better Christian."*

It was crystal clear to all of us that my mother would not return to her home in Florida. Whatever time she had left on this earth, I selfishly wanted every second. Troy and I got her settled in our master bedroom while we moved into the playroom above the garage. This gave her easy access to a bathroom and no stairs to climb. It also placed her next to the living room and the kitchen where she could be a part of our crazy lives. Rarely did she close her door, not wanting to miss out on a single thing. My children's favorite place to hang out was Gammoo's room. There was an assortment of new books, games, art supplies, and a special drawer filled with candy. Annie Lee raced to her bed every day after school. Together, they completed kindergarten homework followed by a sweet treat and a long nap.

There was always an adventure creatively planned for the children. On one occasion she purchased Nerf Super Soaker water guns for everyone and strategically arranged them in the front yard. When the children arrived home from school, it was an all out water war. For another activity, she and Sammy secretly collected worms that had been sizzled into different squiggly shapes on our driveway in the hot sun. They then had a brilliant idea to glue these fried wigglers onto construction paper, making word art. That evening at dinner they presented their masterpiece while laughing hysterically. *So gross!* A creative competition she invented for Annie Lee was called "Say Yes To My Dress." Each contestant would have an allotted amount of time to create an outfit for a doll out of three household objects. For example, they could use a toilet paper tube, grosgrain ribbon, and a napkin. When the time was up, the dolls were judged for the most creatively dressed. Of course, all contestants and judges received sweet treats for participating.

My Journal:
28 October 2010
The last few weeks have been very busy getting my mother settled. A port was implanted surgically in her chest for chemotherapy and her body was marked for radiation treatment. She has also been making sure her affairs are in order. I know this will give her peace of mind when her wishes are documented.

This week has been tough for her, emotionally and physically. Many people have been so kind to offer their services, even free legal counsel. Instead of accepting these thoughtful acts of service, she feels hurt, thinking people are performing out of pity. Lord, please help her embrace this unconditional love.

Some of her sensitivity may also be coming from just feeling lousy. This was her first week to receive chemotherapy and radiation every day.

On top of that, she has battled with vomiting, a yeast infection, an eye infection, inflammation in her lungs, and intermittent fevers. She is now on intravenous antibiotics which I am grateful the doctors are allowing me to administer at home. Thankful that she is finally resting soundly tonight.

Within two months of her diagnosis, a Last Will and Testament and a Health Care Power of Attorney were completed and secured in a lockbox. In the meantime, my sister, Alicia, packed up my mother's house in Panama City, Florida, bringing it all to

Sumter. We spent days sorting through boxes and furniture, tagging
who would be the recipient. Although there was deep sadness in
this process, there was also immense joy since her love language was
giving. This provided her with a sense of autonomy and control
when so much in her life was unpredictable.

The financial and business stressors behind us, it was now
time to focus on my mother's health and making memories every
single day. Soni was a huge blessing during this time. She watched
Benjamin while Troy and the three older children were in school.
This allowed me the opportunity to accompany my mother to all
of her doctor appointments, some lasting hours. Every week, I
snuck new surprises into my bag: Crossword puzzles, board games,
cards, books, and a portable CD/DVD player with earbuds. I loved
watching her face light up when I pulled out item's that triggered
sweet memories like the book *Charlotte's Web* or her favorite classic
movie *My Fair Lady* or the CD featuring Carly Simon's greatest hits.
The entertainment was a perfect distraction during these difficult
circumstances.

My mother had been with us a year when friends and family
began voicing concerns that I may be spreading myself too thin. I
was not sure how to change that since I was a wife of a busy football
coach, a mother of four children who wanted me to play, read to
them, and cheer them on at ballgames or dance performances. I was
a daughter with a very sick mother who needed care every single
day, and a daughter-in-law to a woman I desperately wanted to
please. There were dinners to cook, laundry to fold, and bills to pay.
Honestly, there was no time to feel overwhelmed, and staying as busy
as humanly possible was a coping mechanism to keep from feeling.

My Journal:
8 October 2011
*I had a dream last night that I was floating in a small raft in
the middle of a large body of water. A small pin hole formed
in the bottom of the raft, causing a thin stream of water to
shoot up into the air. No biggie, I put my finger over the hole.
Another hole appeared, placing a separate finger over that
hole, I thought the problem was solved. But before long, I*

was playing the game Twister with all my fingers and toes. I remember feeling exhausted. There were just too many leaks. Then I saw the holes getting bigger and panic set in. I was going to sink. I screamed out to God, "Please help me! I can't do this on my own." I woke up, crying and covered in sweat.

I am empty, exhausted, and drowning. The people-pleaser in me is raging right now and I don't seem to be "pleasing" anyone. I have no balance on who needs me the most. My mother's health is deteriorating and it is all consuming. Yet, my husband and children must feel like they are not a priority. Please help me! I can't do this on my own.

I tried to take a few long walks during the week to exercise, but most importantly, to be alone and listen to music. Music had always been my therapy and I needed it more than ever. I would lace up my sneakers, set my iPod on shuffle, and pray that God would speak through whatever songs played. Some days, I might be found walking with my arms raised in worship while singing loudly. Other days, I might dance or skip down the street. And then others, rivers of tears poured down my face, my grief so raw it was difficult to breathe. *The neighbors must have thought I was losing my mind.*

My Journal:
November 2011
God clearly spoke to me through the lyrics of the songs that played on my walk today. Here is what I heard: "Christon, please don't push me away or tell me that you're okay. You are falling apart and I need you to be real with me. I want your hurt, I want your pain so that I can reach in and touch your wounds. You are NOT alone. Please let me love you."

Oh Lord, you are so right. I am NOT okay. I am empty and numb. It feels like I'm sleepwalking through each day. I need you to fix my broken heart.

He spoke again, "When you think it can't possibly get any harder, I will hold onto you. I will bread crumb the path when you feel like you have lost your way. I can make you laugh when everyone else is crying." Before I had an opportunity to question what those words meant, my eyes were immediately drawn to a bird perched on the lower limb of a tree. The bird's mouth was incessantly opening and closing while it looked directly at me. I took one of my earbuds out to hear the beautiful song the bird must be singing. To my surprise, the noise coming from the bird sounded like it had swallowed the squeaker in a dog toy. I went from tears moments before to uncontrollable laughter.

I don't know where this road leads or how God will heal this pain, but heading toward home, it felt like I was holding hands with my Heavenly Father. His words brought peace and calm to my unsettled soul.

A favorite form of escape for my mother was to be chauffeured in her convertible Toyota Solara. Most of the week we were cooped up in sterile medical environments, so a drive with the top down brought healing and freedom. Breathing the fresh air, feeling the sunshine on our faces and the wind through our hair made us feel alive. If we had to run into a store, my mother thought it was hilarious to walk in with her hair wildly disheveled.

The weaker she became, the more I tried to protect my heart by staying busy. It was much easier to put on my Nurse Hat or focus on marking things off of a "To Do" list. The reality of losing her brought too much pain. There was only one problem, she saw right through this coping mechanism. The more task-oriented I became, the more she called me into her room. It wasn't to give me more to do, but to subtly get me to rest. As I approached her bed she would gently grab my hand, pulling me down to sit, or enticing me into a cozy nap. When she saw worry on my face she would rub my furrowed brow saying "Please smile, I don't want those ugly lines to be frozen on your pretty face."

She spent the last month of her life in bed, drifting in and out of consciousness. During moments of lucidity, it was clear that she knew the end of her life on earth was near. "Chris, please tell the kids that I love them. I love you too honey, but there is nothing else you can do for me. I am comfortable. Please let me go."

My Journal:
2 December 2011
My heart is shredded as I helplessly watch my mother deteriorate. Physically her skin is jaundiced, appetite nonexistent, weight rapidly dropping, and breathing is erratic. Mentally she is aware at times that her "mind is screwy." Some of the things she says concern me, and others make me giggle, like when she asked if I could see the handsome cowboy in the corner of the room with the cute butt.

It is obvious that Annie Lee recognizes these changes. I think she senses my fragility too. She is glued to my side and wants to be my little helper. Each night, Annie climbs into Gammoo's bed and does the following: She reads Gammoo a bedtime story. She rubs lotion on Gammoo's legs. She puts chapstick on Gammoo's lips and then brings her a popsicle. Thank you Lord, for this precious child.

Needed this encouragement today, "Love never gives up, never loses faith, is always hopeful, and endures through every circumstance." (1 Corinthians 13:7 NLT) Lord, I trust that you will help me to bear, believe, hope, and endure all things. Please put my weak eyes on you.

When it became evident that nursing care was needed around the clock, my sister, Alicia, arrived to help. Although the circumstances were excruciating, we made beautiful memories. Noticing significant changes in my mother's breathing pattern, Alicia and I pushed beds together so we could snuggle up beside her. Those last twenty-four hours were spent reminiscing and thanking her for the valuable lessons she taught us. Through tears and laughter, we sang every childhood song we could remember: The Itsy Bitsy Spider, Little Bunny Fu Fu, Twinkle-Twinkle Little Star, and Skidamarink. Finally, when it became too painful to watch her battle between this life and her forever home, we kissed her sweet face and gave her permission to go.

Gammoo and Annie after school

Say Yes to
My Dress Contest

Gammoo's water gun war

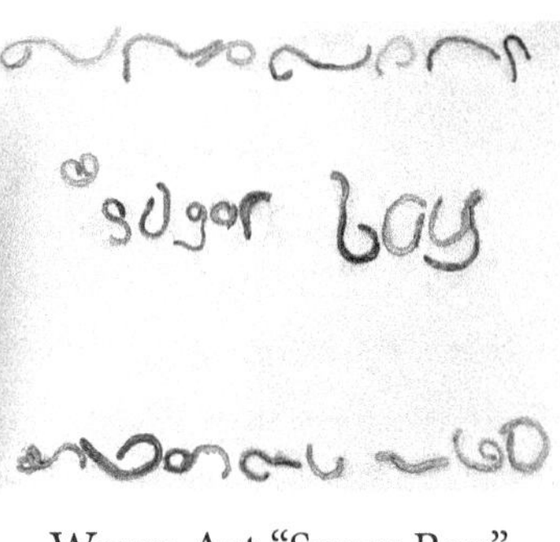

Worm Art "Sugar Boy"

Gammoo playing baseball with the kids in her pajamas

Linda [Gammoo] and Soni [Mama]
Our last Christmas together - 2011

need you now

Plumb

The darkness was devastating. I was not prepared for my body to completely shut down emotionally, mentally, and physically. Emotionally and mentally my heart was so broken that it hurt to breathe. Physically, I was a mess from fifteen months of neglect.

My Journal:
29 December 2011
It has been a rough few weeks. I honestly do not remember the twelve days following my mother's death. She hugged Jesus for the first time on December 14th and then darkness enveloped me. The months of pounding caffeine, poor nutrition, and lack of sleep left me depleted. I was unable to function; my body was screaming- ENOUGH!

High fevers sent me to the doctor where I was prescribed multiple medications for a kidney infection and thrush. Annie Lee climbed in bed with me tonight, saying, "Mommy, you are staying in bed just like Gammoo. Daddy has to bring you food and drinks." I saw the panic on her little face as she tried to process if her mommy was going to die, too. Hugging her tightly, I reassured her that I would be back to normal now that I was on antibiotics.

I could feel the darkness fade as we watched "The Nativity Movie" on Christmas night. This has been a family tradition for years, but for some reason I was mesmerized this year by Mary, the mother of Jesus. I cried and prayed throughout the movie, feeling a renewed strength trickle into my veins. Mary was willing to do whatever God asked, even if people did not understand, or the circumstances brought her personal pain and rejection. I was comforted knowing that her inner strength came, not from the world, but from her Heavenly Father, who walked with her every step of her difficult journey.

Sadness still hits me unexpectedly and not a day passes that I don't want to hug my mom or hear her voice. For now, I have boxed up her pictures, keepsakes, and journals. Seeing them every day was just too painful. "I am worn out from sobbing. All night, I flood my bed with weeping, drenching it with my tears." (Psalm 6:6 NLT)

Five months after my mother's passing, I accepted an invitation to speak to the high school girls at Thomas Sumter Academy. In preparation, I felt led to share a piece of my journey and titled my talk, "This Rough Road." The topic originated from one of my "God Moments" while walking a few months earlier.

A month before my mother's death:
My Journal
November 2011
There are two intersecting streets that I walk regularly, one is a no outlet road and the other curves slightly toward the street where my home is located. Today on my walk, as I mentally processed which direction to go, I looked up and was puzzled at the addition of two new signs on my route. One yellow sign read "Dead End," the other, "Rough Road." Oddly, the song playing on my ipod was about the road we travel being hard. This was profound!

I heard God say, "Christon, you have two choices: you can walk straight ahead on a road which will lead to a dead end or you can turn right on a road that may be rough with some twists and turns, but will lead you home. Although you

When I wrote this in my journal, my mother was alive and I
thought God was preparing me for the difficult road that lay ahead
with her health. Little did I know that our family would be placed on
yet another rough road.

One week after sharing "This Rough Road" message with
high school students, Troy and I took the children to Myrtle Beach
for a Toby Mac concert. As we entered the venue, my phone rang.

145

The physician from our local urgent care called to notify us that Soni, my mother-in-law, was in their office experiencing severe abdominal pain. He was admitting her to the hospital for further testing. I was so confused, she was perfectly fine this morning when we kissed her and said goodbye. Although unsettled and concerned, nothing could have prepared us for the news we would receive twenty-four hours later. Troy's sweet mother was diagnosed with stage 4 pancreatic cancer.

> *My Journal*
> *21 May 2012*
> *Not again! Shock... Disbelief...Why Lord? How could you ask our family to walk this rough road again? The wound from our last loss is still so raw. This is deja vu; the same signs, symptoms, tests, treatments, nurses and doctors. Am I trapped in a nightmare? If so, will someone please wake me up! Did I miss warning signs because I was consumed with my own issues and grief? The guilt...*
>
> *Mind-blowing... this was my Bible reading today, This is what the Lord says: "Stop at the crossroads and look around. Ask for the old, godly way, and walk in it. Travel its path, and you will find rest for your souls. But you reply, 'No, that's not the road we want!' (Jeremiah 6:16 NLT)*

The whole scenario did not make sense, and it certainly was not a road I wanted to traverse again. My "fight or flight" response had been triggered but the wires were jumbled. *Prepare for battle* was the message from my head but my heart was screaming *run and hide!* The conflict left me paralyzed, a total blank slate unable to process how to move forward.

Behind closed doors, after shedding many tears, Troy and I determined that our first step would be to tell the children. *How do you convey hope that maybe this time will be different?* Just five months earlier, they watched, horrified, as a stranger took their Gammoo away from our home in a black car forever. *How would their little brains wrap around more loss and pain?* Due to their age differences, we decided it was best to pull them aside individually. Their tears and questions were heartbreaking, all asking, "Will she die, too?" Troy and I did our best to answer honestly, encouraging them to do all they could to love their Mama each day as if it was her last. Our twelve-year-old, Eli, verbalized his fear of another person dying in our home. Seeing his angst, I immediately began praying that God would prevent this outcome.

Having walked this road before should have made things easier, or at least that is what the enemy kept telling me. The familiarity mixed with uncertainty created a perfect environment to fall into comfortable habits to numb the pain, *busyness*. It was a conundrum, because rest was what I needed most, but resting brought a barrage of unfamiliar and unpredictable symptoms. Many nights I woke up covered in sweat, heart racing, and feeling like I was suffocating. Sharing these health concerns with my family physician, he prescribed Xanax, explaining that my symptoms aligned with anxiety which were causing panic attacks. Embarrassed that I would be seen as weak, ostracized for wanting a quick fix, or not having enough faith, I kept my new medication a secret.

My Journal
10 June 2012
What are you doing, Lord? I am so weak. I am trying so hard to be strong for Troy, the children, and Soni, but in reality I am just a broken little girl who misses her mommy. You must think I can handle all of this, which makes me feel guilty to question you. I have to be honest, this pain is making it hard for me to breathe.

As I read Psalm 62 (NLT) today, I completely related to feeling like a "broken-down wall or a tottering fence." My mind is constantly spinning, trying to plan and protect my heart from what will happen next. This Psalm reminded me that you are "my fortress where I will never be shaken." I must rest and trust that you are with me every step of this difficult journey.

Lord, my hope is that one day these struggles will make me a better wife, mom, and friend. Help me trust that when I am weak, you are strong. (2 Corinthians 12:9-10 NLT) Please don't let go of me! There is no possible way that I can get through this without you.

Our mothers were very different. Troy's mother, Soni, was an introvert, quiet and shy. My mother was an extrovert who knew no stranger. Their differences were apparent in how they dealt with their diagnosis. My mother asked questions, expressed her fears openly, and wanted my feedback. Soni, on the other hand, retreated to her room or found solace in keeping to her normal schedule, which included trips to J.C. Penny or Walgreens. Our immediate and extended family rallied around her over the next eighteen months, accompanying her to doctor's appointments and treatments. We did everything in our power to shower her with love every single day, uncertain how many remained.

> *My Journal*
> *May 2013*
> *Yesterday was Mother's Day, the second one without my mom. I shoved my own emotions to a locked place, choosing to spoil Soni instead. We bought her gifts, made her favorite meal, and Annie Lee even made her cupcakes.*
>
> *Whenever I started to feel anxious or sad, I popped a pill. My head says this is so stupid but my heart says that I can't survive without it. Realistically, I know the relief is only temporary. "Why do I do what I do not want to do?" (Romans 7:15 NLT) I am fearful of becoming an addict like so many of my family members. When I hurt, I want to run to Jesus. Your word says "The Holy Spirit helps us in our weakness." (Romans 8:26 NLT)*
> *Please help me Lord, I am so weak!*

It was painfully obvious that I was emotionally sick, trying to mask it with medications. *How did I get to this place when I had prided myself in being different?* No sooner did I utter this cry for help…help came. Snuggled up in bed one night, Troy gently said, "Honey, are you okay? You're just not the same. The children and I get no quality time, you are too busy doing insignificant things. We need you." At that moment, I felt something inside of me break. A year of bottled up emotions poured out like a rock thrown at a forty-gallon fish tank, shattering its contents to the floor. Everything from my fears of the future, the panic attacks, and medications I had secretly swallowed for a year, all out in the open.

My Journal
June 2013
Let's be honest, I have been a toxic mess for months. Verbalizing the details to Troy was the therapy and accountability that I needed. One of the things he said has really resonated with me. "Life is hard. It is impossible to walk through this life and not be affected by death. There is no escaping it. People are watching us to see if what we believe about Jesus is true. When circumstances suck and the bottom falls out, will we still trust Him? We must keep living and loving."

I have been on autopilot, just sucking air into my lungs to survive. Sadly, believing a lie that medicating would ease the pain. After our talk, I flushed the pills down the toilet, spending two horrible days detoxing my body.

Woke up this morning at sunrise, ready to begin a new chapter in my life. I am so thankful that God makes ALL things new. God is so faithful, here was my Bible reading today: "Give thanks to the Lord, for He is good! His faithful love endures forever. In my distress I prayed to the Lord, and the Lord answered me and set me free. The Lord is for me, so I will have no fear. It is better to take refuge in the Lord than to trust people." (Psalm 118:1-8 NLT)

A former colleague with Troy at Thomas Sumter Academy started a non-profit called The Sounds of Grace. Kipper Ackerman, a talented musician, singer, and storyteller, felt led to bring peace and healing through music to hospitals, healthcare facilities, and special needs classrooms. On many hospital admissions with both my mother and Soni, Kipper would roll her large harp into the small sterile room, blessing us with a few hymns. Her beautiful voice mixed with the angelic sounds of the harp were a welcome distraction from our worries and fears. It made me wonder how many times David must have been summoned to play the harp for King Saul in order to reset his mind, ease anxiety, or comfort his tormented soul. (1 Samuel 16:23 NLT)) Kipper wrote a book titled *From My Harp*, sharing personal testimonies of peace and healing through music.

Grief is so frustratingly unpredictable. A dear friend shared with me that one of the most difficult places for him emotionally after his wife passed away, was Sunday mornings in church. At the time, his words puzzled me. I wasn't sure if this was because church was such an integral part of their lives or if it was the only time he allowed himself to sit still each week. This statement became all too real as I walked those same steps.

I am still not exactly sure why I ran out of church that
Sunday morning. For over twenty-five years the church had been my
safe place. The place where I felt the most understood and accepted.
But there was no denying that our current circumstances had me
floating in uncharted territory. I was a wife and mother of four small
children who needed me, yet I longed to be with my mother. I felt
guilty that I, too, wanted to hug Jesus and escape to a place where
there was no more sorrow, pain, or tears.

By October, Soni was rapidly deteriorating. Despite
intravenous nutrition at home, her weight continued to plummet and
her mental clarity faded. Unlike my mother, Soni had a long-term
care policy which provided in-home nursing services. This was a huge
blessing as she transitioned into requiring twenty-four hours of care
a day. These caregivers became part of our family and I am certain
we would not have survived round two of pancreatic cancer without
them. We also had the support of our extended family in Orlando
who visited often and helped make important decisions about her
care.

One evening after surprising Soni with takeout from her favorite restaurant, Red Lobster, we found her slumped oddly in her recliner. She was unable to follow our basic commands. We called an ambulance and she was admitted to the hospital. Three days later, on what would have been my mother's 69th birthday, Soni hugged Jesus.

My daughter, Annie Lee, asked me recently, "Were you ever angry with God during those years when Gammoo and Mama were so sick?" Choking back tears, I responded, "No honey, I wasn't angry, but I did question Him. Why this road? Why take them both so close together? Why were there so many similarities: pancreatic cancer, Gammoo was diagnosed on Mama's birthday, and Mama passed away on Gammoo's birthday? But more than anything, I was just sad. Sad that Daddy and I no longer had parents and sad that you children no longer had grandparents."

The Lord did not answer those questions, and I am not sure that if He had they would have taken away the pain. Nothing could have erased the palpable loss of their presence. Instead of fixating on the whys, I began to focus on all the ways the Lord had been faithful. We were blessed to have them both live with us, making a lifetime of memories. The photographs taken during these three years are some of our most valued possessions. I smile recalling the ones of Mama reading to the children on our couch or the snapshots of Gammoo teaching them how to do somersaults in the backyard. Many of our prayers were answered along the way, like Eli's fear of another death in our home or the pleading for just a little more time. Our mothers were present when we took our first breath on this earth and we were honored to be present when they took their last.

goodness of god

Jen Johnson

A decade has passed and much has changed in our sweet family. We moved to North Carolina, Troy retired from teaching, and I am now the shortest member of our family. Our oldest two boys are in college, a senior and a freshman, and our younger two children are in high school, a senior and a freshman. I wish I could take credit for perfectly planned parenthood, but clearly this was not the case. Memories of the years of infertility resurface occasionally as I watch in heavenly wonder at how blessed I am to be the mother of these four amazing humans.

There is an old adage that says, "Time heals all wounds." I struggle with this statement as I look at my personal scars: the absence of a father, dysfunctional family members, abuse, loneliness, rejection, infertility, and even the death of loved ones. Time did not heal these deep wounds, Jesus did. The Bible tells us about a gentleman who was paralyzed for thirty-eight years, and a woman who bled for twelve, neither of them received healing by the passing of time. They were healed when Jesus showed up.

Charles Spurgeon, a famous 19th century preacher, once said, "No faith is so precious as that which lives and triumphs through adversity. You would never have known God's strength had His strength not been needed to carry you through." This quote is so true, however, as the years passed, the details of events became fuzzy and forgotten. Naively, I thought journaling would help me remember. The problem was that I never looked back at the things I had written. Instead, I stored them in the attic alongside the box of my mother's journals, which I inherited when she passed away. When the Lord initially nudged me to write my story, I was fearful that my heart was not strong enough to return to those broken places. *Wouldn't it be best to leave the past covered in dust?*

Searching for my purpose in a new chapter of life in North Carolina, I felt lost. I scheduled a meeting with the pastor of our church, in hopes of receiving some discernment. After sharing my heart, the pastor asked, "What was the last thing the Lord told you to do?" *Is he really asking me that question?* My eyes filled with tears and a huge lump formed in my throat leaving me speechless. Patiently, he asked the question again, "Christon, what was the last thing the Lord asked you to do?" Reluctantly I responded, "Write my story."

"The Lord won't give you another assignment until you have completed the one He has asked you to do," he said with compassion. Overhelmed, I left that meeting resolved to finally obey God.

My daughter, Annie Lee, danced four to five days a week at a studio forty-five minutes from where we lived. In lieu of driving home, I sat in the parking lot, climbed to the back of my Ford Expedition and slowly began to write. Miraculously, when I finally obeyed the Lord, my tsunami of fears were quickly erased and replaced by the presence of Jesus. I saw glimpses of Him every step of the way: A devotion or Bible verse that undoubtedly God picked for me. Songs whose lyrics were a balm for my soul and seemed to be written with me in mind. The encouraging words from a friend that were surprisingly right on time. Looking back gave me countless opportunities to hear His voice again in so many forgotten and unexpected places. Time may not have healed my wounds, but it definitely revealed the goodness of God.

There is no longer fear of the past, for remembering has become a beautiful gift. There is no longer fear of the future, for I have a faithful friend and forever Father who has always been singing over me. (Zephaniah 3:17) Having a relationship with Jesus changed everything, giving me the freedom to be different and the confidence to sing a new song. (Psalm 59:16-17)

Sorting the journals

$\heartsuit$

Writing in the back of the car

My people - 2021

it's been you

Christon Kessinger

(singing to daddy)
Don't turn away and say goodbye
My heart is breaking, you know why
Give me your hand, say you'll stay
Darkness surrounds me
Who will take this pain away?

Here I am
Singing a song to your soul
I will love you forever
In me you can be whole
Follow me and you will never be alone
Hold my hand, I'll lead you home

(singing to mommy)
Don't turn away, I see you cry
It's crushing my spirit and you know why
Give me your hand, we'll be ok
When the darkness surrounds us
Who will take the pain away?

Here I am
Singing a song to your soul
I will love you forever
In me you can be whole
Follow me and you will never be alone
Hold my hand, I'll lead you home

Don't turn away, and hide your shame
Your heart is breaking, and I know why
Give me your hand and I will stay
When the darkness surrounds you
I will take the pain away

Here I am
Singing a new song to your soul
You're no longer orphaned
In me you are whole
Follow me and you will never be alone
Hold my hand, I'll lead you home

(singing to the Lord)
You won't turn away or say goodbye
Forever my Father, you are mine
It's been you, singing to my soul
I am no longer broken
In you I am whole

Here I am
Singing a song to you Lord
I will love you forever
In you I am whole
I'll follow you and I'll never be alone
Hold my hand and lead me home
Hold my hand and lead me home

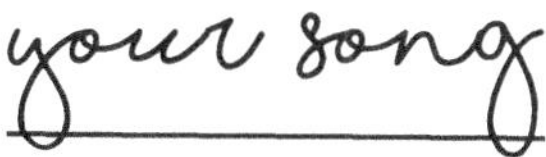

Our personal stories are a song to the world. They sing the praises of a Heavenly Father who was, is, and will always be present in our lives. (Psalm 66) The prerequisite for sharing them has nothing to do with being famous, the number of followers you have, or a seminary degree. Rather it has everything to do with being obedient. God uses the most unlikely and ordinary people to make His name famous. Now, it's your turn.

- Read Psalm 139:13-18. Do you believe that your story began here? Is there anything in these verses that makes you pause? Explain.

- How have your relatives (grandparents, parents, aunts, uncles, siblings) influenced you emotionally, physically, and spiritually?

- Did their words or actions make a significant impact on your life? Were they positive, negative, or confusing? Did you feel heard and valued? How did those experiences influence your life today? Explain.

- Do you want to continue on the same paths as the people on your family tree? Why? You may resemble them but you can be different. This is a choice, you can sing a new song.

- Have you ever tried to numb pain, disappointment, or rejection in order to bury it deep inside? (examples: unhealthy relationships, substance abuse, body image issues, busyness) What did you learn from that experience and how can you cope differently next time?

- What was your first introduction to the church or faith? Was it positive, negative, or confusing? Explain.

- If you have a relationship with Jesus, when did it begin?

- When you remember significant moments of your life, do you see Jesus? Explain.

- Are there any particular songs that trigger a memory for you? What are they?

- Read Jeremiah 29:11-14. How can these promises be applied to your story — past, present, future?

———————

I would love to hear your story: tcesab6@gmail.com

shout outs

jesus, thank you for pushing me out of my comfort zone and showing up every step of the way. My heart is filled with gratitude for your prompting, persistence and patience. Because of you I am different and will sing a new song, even if it's off key.

troy, thank you for loving me and always seeing the beauty in my scars. You steady me.

eli, sammy, annie lee and benjamin, I love being your mommy! If you read this book, LOL, I hope you will see the goodness of God.

theresa, tabitha and cindy, I would have hit delete years ago if it weren't for your prayers and encouragement. I have asked the Lord to add extra jewels to your crowns for the hours you have spent listening, reading and crying with me throughout this project. Thank you for reminding me that we serve a BIG God and with Him, nothing is impossible.

mom, I miss you every single day. I am so grateful that you wrote your highs and lows for over five decades. These journals help me hear your voice and have been a lifeline to me since you've been gone. xxoo

masterpiece for eternity

In the process of writing this book, Stephanie Thomasson, a beautiful nineteen-year-old, unexpectedly went home to be with Jesus. For two years she had been involved in the bible study held weekly at my home. Stephanie's favorite bible verse was "For we are God's masterpiece. He has created us anew in Christ Jesus, so we can do the good things he planned for us long ago." (Ephesians 2:10 NLT) Her parents, Greg and Cindy, have set up a donor advised fund called Masterpiece For Eternity. This fund supports various ministries that Stephanie was passionate about. Proceeds from this book will be donated to this fund.

https://linktr.ee/christonkessinger

come and listen,
all you who fear god,
and i will tell you
what he did for me.

(Psalm 66:16 NLT)